GENESIS
REVISITED

GENESIS
REVISITED

A Revolutionary New Solution
to the Mystery of Man's Origins

Glenn G. Strickland

 THE DIAL PRESS · *New York*

Published by
The Dial Press
1 Dag Hammarskjold Plaza
New York, New York 10017

Manufactured in the United States of America
First printing
Design by Dennis J. Grastorf

Library of Congress Cataloging in Publication Data

Strickland, Glenn G.   1917–
Genesis revisited.

Includes index.
1. Human evolution. 2. Social evolution. I. Title.
GN281.4.S87   573.2   79-4528

Dedicated to the women in my life:
Leslie and Dorothy

CONTENTS

INTRODUCTION

ANTHROPOLOGY includes the study of the origins of the human species. However, there is remarkably little in this area to study. In the almost a hundred years since the death of Charles Darwin, anthropologists have made little progress in determining why humans are what we are. Why did our species lose its body hair? Why do we walk erect? How did intelligence evolve? Except for a few guesses, you cannot find answers to these questions in books written on anthropology by professional anthropologists. This book, though written by an amateur in anthropology, answers these questions and many more.

The immediate and natural reaction to statements like the one above is to ask: If the professionals in a field of science cannot solve their problems, how can an amateur? This is a good question, with a simple and natural answer. So before we go on, we will answer it and let the chips fall where they may.

If we compare the advances made in anthropology in the past hundred years with the advances made in the other sciences in the same time span, we can see that anthropology has remained almost at a standstill, while the other sciences have shot ahead at an ever-increasing rate. It is true, of course, that a few prehuman fossils have been found now and then, and these finds receive great publicity. But these few finds have not enabled anthropologists to answer the basic

I

questions. Anthropologists have not been able to fit these new "missing links" into our family tree. Far from shedding new light on our past, these new finds all add more unanswered questions. The mystery of our past is darker now than it seemed to be when Darwin was alive.

If the facts are faced, it can be seen that anthropologists are failing to solve their problems while other scientists are solving theirs. This suggests that anthropologists are not using the same methods to solve problems that other scientists use. A very small bit of research will confirm this suspicion. When faced with problems, anthropologists try to solve them with speculations. Other scientists solve their problems with calculations.

Solving problems is part of the business of being a scientist. There is really no excuse for speculating when there are methods available to solve problems without having to guess. Of course most of the problems of the past are nonnumerical problems. But that should not make any difference to scientists.

We all know that there are techniques such as algebra and calculus for solving numerical problems. We may not all know that there are equivalent techniques for solving nonnumerical problems. But it is not the business of most of us to know. Scientists, however, should know of Boolean algebra, modeling, and all those other techniques that can solve nonnumerical problems by calculation. Maybe anthropologists know about these techniques, but their writings indicate they don't use them. I do not know why.*

Boolean algebra was invented about a hundred and fifty years ago. Charles Darwin himself could have used it. Maybe he did. It is a technique used to translate sentences such as you are now reading into symbols and then to check the resultant equations for truth. Darwin might have used this

---

* These problem-solving techniques are not part of the required curriculum for a degree in anthropology, but that is no excuse either.

technique to check his basic theory. But if he did, it certainly seems as if he was both the first and the last anthropologist to do so.

There you have both the reason for the relative stagnation in anthropology and the reason that an amateur might be able to solve some of the problems that have been unsolved for a hundred years. Anthropologists may be experts in anthropology, but their writings prove that they are novices at problemsolving. The author of this book is an amateur in anthropology, but he is an expert at problem solving. He is a retired operations research analyst.

The techniques of operations research solve both numerical and nonnumerical problems. Their use is not restricted to any field any more than the use of simple arithmetic is. These problem-solving techniques have been used in agriculture, ballistics, communications, and right on through the alphabet to zymurgy, the chemistry of beer- and wine-making. The only limitation to the use of operations research techniques is that in the field of application, the actions and reactions must be subject to laws, natural or otherwise. This limitation thus excludes from the purview of operations research techniques only fine arts and magic.

Evolution is not a fine art. We did not evolve by magic, either. Evolution is a natural process, and all natural processes proceed in accordance with natural laws. Therefore it was not hard to apply the methods of operations research to the problems of human evolution to get calculated answers. This is not to say that the techniques made the problems easier to solve. The problems were still complex and tedious. But answers were obtained by calculations and without the need for guessing.

Starting with the same data available years ago to any anthropologist, the methods of operations research produced a series of rather simple answers to the complex problems of the past. When strung together, these simple answers make up a coherent and straightforward account of human prehistory, covering the last twenty million years or so in fair detail. This history differs greatly from accounts of our past that are based on speculations. But since this history is based on calculations, it can be recreated by anyone with the skills who cares to take the trouble.

For an analogy, you can give samples of a mineral to a number of chemists, and the independent reports you get back will yield virtually identical values for the chemical composition of the mineral, its physical and chemical properties, and the forces and conditions required to create it. These reports will agree because they will all be based on calculations and consideration of natural laws. You may consider this book a report on the evolution of *Homo sapiens sapiens*. (The wise, wise men, as we like to call ourselves.) Still you are free to call this book theory if you like, at least until the calculations have been independently replicated.

This report shows that human evolution, like the evolution of every animal species, was the natural and inevitable consequence of environmental pressures and the operation of natural laws. Our remote ancestors had no choice but to become what we are. This analysis accounts for the major changes from our apelike ancestors into modern humans. It accounts for all prehuman fossils and locates them in our family tree. Most importantly, the book shows how many of our modern troubles stem from the forced evolution of our ancestors. The account is not hard to read—there is no further mention of operations research. This story of our long lost past, though, is such a strange and sometimes ugly story that many will not want to believe it and so will not believe it—at least not at first. At that, our prehistory is no more ugly or strange than our known history. Regardless, history cannot be changed and neither can prehistory. All we can do about our past is try to understand it and perhaps profit from the knowledge.

*

The Moving Finger writes; and, having writ,
Moves on: nor all thy Piety or Wit
Shall lure it back to cancel half a Line,
Nor all thy Tears wash out a word of it.

(*Verse 51*, The Rubáiyát of Omar Khayyám)

CHAPTER 1

THE JIGSAW PUZZLE
OF THE PAST

WHY ARE WE HUMANS shaped as we are? Why do we walk erect, and why do we have so little body hair? Why do men have beards and women curves? You will find the answers to these questions and many more in the following chapters.

This book is an outline of the prehistory of the human species, concentrating on the last twenty million years. It includes the major steps in our evolution, giving the how, when, where, and why for the changes from our animal ancestors into ourselves. We may like to think that whatever we are is the result of our own efforts, and in a way this is true; but the raw material each of us started with is a legacy from our ancestors of millions of years back. Basically we are what we are because of the conditions that our ancestors encountered and the things that they had to do to stay alive.

"Know thyself!" was an inscription on a Delphic temple, and these words have been repeated by numerous philosophers since. Alexander Pope said, "The proper study of mankind is man." These expressions are good advice, but, as is so often the case with good advice, the advice is meaningless.

No man is an island. No man can fully understand himself unless he understands all mankind. This understanding necessarily includes a knowledge of how humans came to be what we are. However, the specifics of our origins have been mysteries ever since people started thinking about the subject.

Finally, along came Darwin. Did the mysteries clear up? Not much. Darwin provided us with the fundamental fact that the remote ancestor of humans was some ancient apelike creature. Just this one fact and practically nothing more.

Today we are not much farther along. We have an apelike ancestor on one side of a gap and we have ourselves on the other. This gap is twenty million years wide. This book is the first to bridge the gap. The view from the bridge is stupendous.

Let's return briefly to Charles Darwin. When Darwin died, he was honored by burial in Westminster Abbey. After the funeral, it is related, an elegantly dressed young peer approached Thomas Huxley, one of the pallbearers, and inquired, "Is it possible that Darwin was correct?" Huxley replied, "Of course he was correct!" The peer looked troubled. Then he whispered, "Couldn't he have kept his theory to himself?"

The answer to the peer's second question is that it wouldn't have made much difference had Darwin kept his ideas to himself. All the facts needed for the theory of evolution were already known to a rather large number of persons. You might say that evolution was an idea whose time had come. If Darwin had not put these facts together as he did, someone else would have. In fact, a Mr. A. R. Wallace did— not before Darwin formulated his ideas, but before Darwin got around to publishing them.

Since Darwin's time a number of discoveries that relate to the specifics of human evolution have been made. These new facts are not particularly complicated, and they are known to a large number of people. You could say that the specifics of human evolution is information whose time has come, because when these new facts plus some old ones are put together like the bits of a giant jigsaw puzzle, most of the mysteries of human evolution immediately clear up.

This has not been done before because of just one impediment. All the required bits of knowledge are not to be found in any one field of science. Note that I did not say that *all* of the facts are known to a large number of people. A large number of people know some of the facts, and a large number of others know other facts. No man is an island, and no science is either. However, there is a regrettable human tendency to try to make sciences islands. The workers in one field sometimes seem to go out of their way to ignore information provided in others. This book is the first to bring all the pertinent facts together.

Strictly speaking, the mysteries of human evolution are problems for anthropologists. But the bits of facts in the field of anthropology alone are far too meager to assemble and suggest any idea of the big picture, no matter how these bits are stretched or twisted. If, however, we add to the bits of facts in anthropology some bits from geography, geology, and a few other fields, the jigsaw puzzle of our past can be assembled without trouble. Furthermore, it does not take an expert in anthropology or an expert in anything else to put the picture together. Because you have read this far, you can do it, probably better than many experts whose minds are cluttered with dogma that they confuse with data. All it takes is some aptitude for jigsaw puzzles or a liking for mystery stories.

Here is the first bit of fact for our jigsaw puzzle. All animals, including humans, are what they are because of the natural forces exerted on the species by long exposure to some environment. Ducks have web feet because their ancestors lived for millions of years in some wet places where web feet were an aid to survival. Of course the wet environment itself did not create the web feet. The first preduck with web feet was a genetic accident. The environment merely favored the survival of this first lucky accident and its progeny that bred true. Evolution is as simple as that. Each and every feature of every species, humans included, stems from lucky accidents that gave their possessors some advantage in the grim business of survival *in the environment inhabited by the species at that time.*

From the above, it is evident that a knowledge of the environment where a species evolved can be a big help in understanding the reasons for the features of that species. Conversely, the features of a species are clues to the type of environment preferred by that species.

We do not have any particular trouble in accounting for the special features of penguins because we know that penguins evolved in the Antarctic. But if we did not have this knowledge and started an investigation of penguins with a blind and unshakable belief that penguins evolved in the Sahara, we would have considerable trouble in determining why penguins are what they are. It would seem that natural laws were violated—that is, that penguins were created by magic.

A good number of serious anthropologists have a firm and unshakable belief that humans evolved in Africa. This is only a belief, and beliefs are not necessarily facts. Many other anthropologists admit they do not know where humans evolved, and they have pointed out that many of the special features of humans could not have resulted from the environment of Africa any more than the special features of penguins could have resulted from the environment of the Sahara.

If this were not enough, there is a time problem to consider. The environment of Africa was not an environment conducive to the rapid evolution of any of the native animals positively known to have resided in Africa for the past few million years. We have the bones of the animals to prove it. It is also known that our species evolved extremely rapidly in the past few million years.

Should we assume that one species—ours—was somehow favored by nature so that it evolved rapidly, while all of the other animals in the same environment evolved very slowly? Well, some people are able to believe just that.

However, I am pleased to report that many anthropologists are convinced that, regardless of where our species evolved, it could not have been Africa. It was someplace else. This book will locate that someplace else. It will be shown that the environment of that someplace else could (and did) have the characteristics that would produce all of the special features that distinguish humans from all other animals.

Please do not jump ahead now to see where it was that our ancestors evolved into us. You will find out soon enough. Furthermore, you must keep it in mind that *Homo sapiens* is a very strange and unusual species. It should be self-evident that the environment required to produce such a strange species would be rather unusual. Not that the environment that produced us was not strictly natural; it was. But it was still so unusual that you should read over the preliminary data first or you may find it hard to accept our birthplace.

For an analogy, think of the differences in the environments that produced diamonds and graphite. Chemically the two substances are identical. Both are naturally occurring crystalline forms of carbon. Both were created by natural forces, but by different intensities of natural forces.

It is the strangeness of the environment that changed our ancestors from apes into us that has prompted this jigsaw puzzle presentation of our prehistory. All of the facts will be laid out before you without evasion or sleight-of-hand tricks and you will be able to see how the bits fit together without violating any of the natural laws affecting the evolution of animals.

However, solving a jigsaw puzzle is not like writing a history. Most histories start at some date and proceed smoothly to a terminal date. But we do not solve jigsaw puzzles that way. First we turn all of the puzzle bits right side up. Then we make a preliminary sorting of the bits. All of the pieces with a straight edge go into one pile, as they are probably boundaries. The other bits are sorted into piles by color and pattern. Then we start work.

But not on the big picture. Not yet. First we make some preliminary subassemblies from the bits in one pile and then in another. After we have a number of these subassemblies, we arrange them on a table, and then perhaps we can get some idea of the big picture. After we have that, the work goes faster. Finally we go back and forth over the picture, plugging up the holes with the leftover bits. Even if there are some missing pieces at the end, we can pretty well predict what those missing bits will look like if they are ever found.

The next three chapters are a presentation of the bits of facts that we need to get started with in our assembly of the picture of our past. These bits are not too complicated. You may already be familiar with them. However, bear with us, because all of these bits will be needed sooner or later.

I promise that you will not be subjected to listings of the complicated names given to the various types of prehumans or to detailed descriptions of the minute differences in their bones. You can get all of these details elsewhere, and since we have twenty million years to cover, we cannot include much that is available elsewhere. Still, if you do go out and get these details, you will be able to see for yourself how they all fit into the framework that will be provided by this pre-history.

It should help us to know where our species is going to know where it has been in the past. Those who do not know history, it is said, are doomed to repeat it. Humans have been repeating their known history over and over. But then we know our history for only just a few thousand years back. This twenty-million-year addition to our known history may help our species get out of its rut. Now, if you are ready to know where humans came from, as well as how and why, go on to the next chapter and dive into our past.

CHAPTER 2

HUMANITY'S HERITAGE

T HE HISTORY of our species really begins with the first
creation of life on this planet. However, this is two
billion years or so farther back than we will try to go; the details of the early portion of our prehistory are available elsewhere. This book will begin about twenty million years ago,
when the mystery of our separation from the apes began, and
will concentrate on only the transition period.

Since our remote ancestors were animals, it is pertinent to
start with the methods used to trace the evolution of animals.
The easiest and best way is by direct comparison of the bones
of modern animals with the bones of their progressively more
ancient ancestors. You can find many exhibits of such sets of
bones in our museums. For example, one exhibit has the
bones of modern horses at one end. At the other end are the
bones of a four-toed, fox-sized creature we call *Eohippus*
(Dawn horse). From just the sets of bones at the ends of the
exhibit we could not be sure that *Eohippus* was the ancestor of
modern horses. But we have the bones of all the intermediate
creatures that present the entire chain of evolution without
any missing links. Therefore there is no doubt that *Eohippus*
was the ancestor of the modern horse.

The exhibits showing the evolution of horses look straightforward and simple. They are. At least they are now; but it
was not always so. The paleontologists had some troubles as-
sembling the first set of bones. They had the same kind of
troubles that now bother the anthropologists who are trying

to assemble sets of bones to show our evolution. So let's look at these troubles.

Eohippus lived in North America. Some of his descendants moved to Asia. Those that remained in America became extinct. At first it was believed that horses evolved in the Old World. The ancestry of horses was traced backward to Asia. Then, from just the fossil evidence alone, it seemed that horses suddenly appeared in Asia without having had ancestors. This seeming fact prompted a number of wild theories, amongst them the supernatural.

But horses came from America to Asia quite naturally. They walked. You cannot walk that route today, but you could have at several different times in the past. The sea bottom did not rise up. Instead the waters fell, creating a land bridge between the continents. Each of the recurring ice ages locked up so much water in the glaciers that the level of all the oceans fell considerably. The last ice age, which ended only twelve thousand years ago, caused the sea level to be just about two hundred and forty feet below where it is now. The Bering Sea is not that deep. In the ice ages, animals crossed the land bridge in both directions. Horses and camels went west. Men and mastodons went east.

The horses that stayed behind in North America, the camels too, and a number of other rather large animals, suddenly vanished about eight thousand years ago. Why? Those species were hunted to extinction. The Indians at that time were pretty good hunters. But they were simultaneously too instinctive and too intelligent for their own good. All nature functions as a sort of capitalistic system. Every creature is motivated to obtain the greatest reward for the least expenditure of effort. The preferential prey of every hunter, animal or human, is the largest prey animal that can be killed without too much trouble or danger. The Indians of that time obtained the most meat with the least trouble by stampeding whole herds over the edge of cliffs. Today there are vast bone piles at the foot of many cliffs that attest to this practice. Some few bones show that the animals were cut up for human food. Some few bones show evidence of feasting by scavengers. Most of the bones show only the effects of this fall.*

This and similar hunting techniques reduced the animal populations rapidly. The few scattered survivors were unable to form and maintain a viable group size. Conservationists the early Indians were not. But then neither were any other type of human or prehuman.

The entry of any new type of *Homo* into every new environment coincides with the extinction of several native animal species, usually rather large animals that can be safely killed. Don't think humans are unique in this, either. All predators kill far more than they can consume, but only when the killing is not too much trouble, because killing is usually hard work. But when the killing is easy, killers kill for the fun of killing. A single fox or mink will wipe out an entire flock of chickens. A single lion will kill fifty or more sheep in one night. It is the nature of every creature to enjoy doing what it must do to survive.

We have found far too few of the relics of our ancestors to be able to construct an exhibit showing the evolution of our species such as we have for horses. Also, when we go back more than a couple of million years, the relics are rather doubtful. There are not just a few missing links; whole sections of the chain are missing. Still, those relics that we do have point backward in time to some completely apelike creature who lived in Africa twenty million years ago.

Let's imagine we have a time machine and can take a trip to the Africa of twenty million years ago. If we could, we might be surprised. Not because it was so different, but because it was so much the same. We would have no trouble recognizing the ancestors of modern African animals. We have sets of bones in our museums that prove that the native African animals had all evolved to essentially their present size and shape a lot longer than just twenty million years ago.

---

* See Paul Martin, "Pleistocene Overkill," in *Natural History*, Dec. 1967.

Technically speaking, we would not see any chimpanzees back there. But we would see some creatures that we might think were chimpanzees. These were the ancestors of modern chimpanzees. We call them Proconsul. There are no "missing links" between chimpanzees and Proconsul; the differences are too slight. The chimpanzees have arms that are a little longer. The chimpanzee fangs are a trifle longer too. However, Proconsul's fangs were nothing to trifle with.

The differences between the two are so trivial that it is hard to see why they are considered as a separate species. There is just one good reason, but this reason is not based on anatomy. It is the fact that the relics of our ancestors point back to Proconsul as having been the common ancestor of both chimpanzees and humans. It is more palatable, even for scientists, to say that humans descended from some apelike creature called Proconsul than to come right out and state that humans are descended from chimpanzees.

If we start with Proconsul and try to climb down our family tree, we immediately run into trouble. First there is a two- or three-million-year gap. Then there is a creature called Ramapithecus. We don't know much about either Proconsul or Ramapithecus. But we do know enough to know that if Ramapithecus is descended from Proconsul, there are several "missing links" between the two. The relics of Ramapithecus have been found in France, India, China, and Africa. In each case, Ramapithecus, like the horses in Asia, seems to have suddenly appeared without having any direct ancestors.

We have bones of a number of creatures that are possibly links between Ramapithecus and us. But in this case, too, there are several "missing links" between them and Ramapithecus or any other creature. All of these creatures have long and difficult names and even to list them here would unnecessarily complicate this narration. However, they do have a place in our prehistory, and we will fit them in later. Fossils are facts, and facts cannot be ignored.

Since we run into a block trying to come down from Proconsul to us, let's return to our time trip to the Africa of twenty million years ago. Back then, it is true, we would have had little trouble recognizing the ancestors of modern African animals. But we would have seen a number of animals that might have puzzled us because quite a few species have become extinct between then and now. For example, roughly two million years ago, several species of African animals quite suddenly became extinct. These species included a type of giant pig, a giant sheep as big as a modern cow, and a few others. All were large animals. Scientists are unable to account for the natural process that exterminated large animals and spared the small, except that most of them think the arrival in Africa of *Homo habilis* (handy man), an early type of human, at about the same time was more than a coincidence.

Let's shift our assembly of facts to another field. All animals are related if you go back far enough. Chimpanzees are our closest animal cousins. Apparently, vice versa, too. Blood serum typings, comparative anatomy, common diseases, and a thousand other facts prove it. Since we are such close kin, we should have a common ancestor not too far back. Proconsul was very probably that common ancestor.

There are many missing links between Proconsul and us. But under some circumstances, missing links may be skipped over. To skip over the missing links in our ancestry, our scientists borrowed one of the techniques used by modern genealogists to skip over missing generations when they are tracing the family tree of modern humans. Let's suppose that a genealogist has this problem. He cannot find any record of a few generations of a family. But as sometimes happens, the family has a unique heirloom that can be traced. For example, half a gold coin—with a family tradition that some ancestor cut the coin in two and gave half to his brother. If the genealogist can locate the other half of the coin in a family that has the same tradition and knows its ancestry, the genealogist is fairly safe in skipping over the missing generations. Surely the families were one family before the date on the coin.

Exactly the same technique strongly indicates that Proconsul is our ancestor as well as the ancestor of chimpanzees. Ordinarily we do not think of animals having possessions, much less unique heirlooms, but most of them do. The unique heirlooms possessed by most animals are their lice.

Lice are tiny bugs that infest the hair or feathers of most living creatures. Lice can be considered animals, and, like all animals, lice evolve to become better adapted for life in their environment. But the lice have paid a price for their evolution. Long ago the lice evolved to be so adapted to specific environments that they cannot live in any other. Furthermore, as the host animals evolved, their lice evolved along with them.

Some of the evolution of the lice was mechanical. Their claws changed shape to become better at grasping the hairs or feathers of the hosts. But that isn't the only way that the lice evolved. Lice are bloodsuckers, and their digestive systems evolved so that they can live only on the blood of their hosts. Human lice, for example, will try to survive on hogs and other animals, but they just cannot make it for more than a few days.

Incidentally, human hairs come in a variety of sizes and shapes. Straight hairs have a circular cross section, curly hairs are oval, and, under a microscope, kinky hairs look like flat ribbons. Different varieties of lice have evolved with claws to fit each shape of hair. So humans have many varieties of lice, even though, technically speaking, there are only two species who can live on humans. We can swap our lice for chimpanzee lice, and, except for some mechanical troubles in holding on, the lice are just as happy in either environment. But we cannot swap lice with any other animal, not even with our second cousins, the gorillas.

We know that chimpanzees are descended from Proconsul. Chimpanzees inherited their lice from Proconsul. But whom did we inherit our lice from if not from Proconsul? Of course it might not have been Proconsul who so generously divided his lice between his descendants. It might have been the next creature upstream in time from Proconsul. However, if that were so, it was so far back that the lice would have had time to modify their digestive systems as well as their claws, because human blood and chimpanzee blood, while similar, are far from identical—even if our lice cannot tell the difference.

Let's shift to the facts in another area. Our prehistory is also the story of our evolution. It is necessary to touch on the mechanics of evolution because there is much misconception in that area. Actually evolution is very simple. Evolution is a change in an animal species. This change comes about in exactly the same way that a rancher produces a change in his herd of cattle. First he gets a bull with the desired characteristics. The bull is protected, fed, sheltered, watered, and given access to the cows. Other bulls are denied access. The descendants who do not inherit the desired characteristics are culled out. In a few generations the entire herd has changed to have the desired characteristics. *The herd has evolved.*

In nature the same thing happens to change the characteristics of a species. First some individual shows up with some desirable feature—something that gives this individual an advantage in the grim business of survival. The appearance of the feature in the first individual is a genetic accident. The characteristics of a species are encoded in the DNA molecules present in every cell, and DNA is extremely resistant to change. But sometimes the DNA furnished in a fertilized egg (ovum) has the parts of the molecule somewhat rearranged. This will produce an offspring with some different feature. If this different feature gives an advantage, it is a rare accident. But it is no accident that this feature will eventually spread and be common to the entire species. It is like the house advantage in all gambling places that insures that in the long run the house will be the only winner. Any advantage, no matter how slight, will eventually become common to a species. Equally, any disadvantage, no matter how slight, eventually results in extinction. But it takes a long time. In the meantime, the environment may change, and a feature that is an advantage in one environment may be a handicap in another.

For example, a few thousand years ago, some little fish were trapped in a stream in a cave in Kentucky. Today the descendants of those fish are blind and eyeless. The eyes that vanished from these fish did not atrophy from disuse in the species. The eyes are a feature that are encoded in the fish DNA, and DNA is totally oblivious to the environment.

At first every generation of fish that was born in the cave had perfectly functional eyes. This would have continued forever, too, except that sometimes, for imperfectly understood reasons, the DNA in an individual does change. A few blind fish are born every year in our hatcheries. These fish promptly die, but when an eyeless fish was hatched in the cave, it did not die because it had a decided advantage.

The eyes of the normal fish were not just useless in the Stygian darkness; the eyes were a handicap. Fish eyes are large, protruding, easily damaged organs. The fish with normal eyes were forced to move slowly in their quest for food. The first lucky fish hatched without eyes could move rapidly. So could his or her descendants. There was only a limited amount of food in the tiny environment of the cave, and the fast-moving, eyeless fish got it all. The unlucky others starved to death. This change in the fish was a true evolutionary step, typical of all evolutionary steps—the major difference being that compared with most, the small size of the environment produced a very rapid evolution.

Note that the above illustration shows that evolution can, and does, work in either direction. It can make a feature appear, get larger, get smaller, or vanish, depending on the circumstances. What is required is only that the direction of the change be in the direction of more efficient survival. If a change in environment merely makes some features useless, the features will not vanish. This is a law of evolution, "Dollo's law," if you care to look it up. Dollo's law is sometimes summarized as "evolution is irreversible" or "evolution is a one-way street." But even if evolution is a one-way street, it can take sharp U-turns that may look like, but are not, reversals.

It should also be noted from the above that it is a change in an environment that prompts a change in a species. After a species has become adapted to an environment, further evolution is generally very slow. In the essentially unchanging environment of the oceans we find our oldest species, such as sharks and sea turtles.

Up to now we have been speaking of "fast" evolution or "slow" evolution. It is time to make our terms more precise. First let's see what the exhibits that show the evolution of animals can tell us. They tell us that evolution usually takes a long time. Our cousins the chimpanzees took twenty million years to evolve only a tiny bit away from Proconsul. This is generally true of all animals, everywhere in the world. The experts in animal evolution tell us that, in a normal environment, it takes a minimum of six million years for an animal species to evolve into a new species, but generally it takes much longer.

A "normal" environment means just what it sounds like it means. If a species lives in an essentially unchanging, continent-sized environment, it lives in a normal environment, and the time requirement applies. This is true regardless of the size of the individuals, applying as much to elephants as to sparrows. And, of course, lice. Incidentally, the environment of Africa has been a normal environment for the past twenty million years and longer. True, there have been a number of climatic changes, but these did not last long enough, nor were they severe enough, to have any particular effect on the native animals. We have the bones to prove it.

There is no argument that there are about two dozen links in the chain of evolution between Proconsul and us. However, *if our species had evolved in a normal environment, there would have been time for only three.*

Anthropologists ignore this fact.
Other scientists would not.

Because of the way evolution works, it is a physical impossibility for our species to have evolved as much as we have *if* our direct line of ancestors had lived in a normal environment. This should be an indisputable fact, and it is the refusal to accept this fact that is responsible for the vast amount of confusion about our prehistory. Yet it is well known that there are quite a number of rather special environments where evolution can be rapid. The environment of the cave fish is one of them.

Let me jump ahead in this history. The actual spot where our species resided during the time that our ancestors rapidly evolved away from our ape cousins has been discovered and rediscovered in the last few years. The discoveries were made by scientists, too. However, there are many fields of science. Those scientists who discovered our birthplace were not looking for it. When they found it, they reported their discoveries in technical papers and in the popular press. But they did not recognize their discovery for what it was. Well, why should they have? One must combine various bits of knowledge from separate fields to make the recognition. It is something like the problem of the horse bones in Asia. The answer as to how the horses got to Asia required some knowledge of the geological history of the world not known at first to paleontologists.

We are going to locate the specific geographical area where our ancestors lived while they evolved from apes into humans. But we want to recognize that place when we get to it. Therefore, before we get out our maps, we should assemble all of the data currently known about places that produce rapid evolution in general and a place that could produce *us* in particular. Fortunately, much of this work has already been done. It was done by a recognized authority in evolution, too.

CHAPTER 3

THE SEARCH FOR
OUR BIRTHPLACE

ABOUT A HUNDRED and fifty years ago, Charles Darwin visited the Galápagos islands. There he made many of the
observations that later led to his theory of evolution. It was
also there that he formulated the mandatory requirements for
a place of rapid evolution. Darwin's conclusions have never
been seriously questioned, and since our species broke all
known speed records in its rapid evolution, we will review
what Darwin found. To give you some flavor of Darwin's
writing, here are some quotations from *The Origin of Species*
(Harvard Classics Edition, Volume II, P. F. Collier & Son,
1909):

> (Referring to birds on islands close to the mainland) Any ten-
> dency to modification will also have been checked by in-
> tercrossing with the unmodified immigrants.
> (Referring to islands far from the mainland) Hence, when in
> former times an immigrant first settled on one of the islands,
> or when it subsequently spread from one to the other, it
> would undoubtedly be exposed to different conditions in the
> different islands, for it would have to compete with a different
> set of organisms. . . . Undoubtedly, if one species has any
> advantage over another, it will in a brief time wholly or in
> part supplant it. . . .

The specific birds that aroused Darwin's interests were a
number of varieties of finches, now called Darwin's finches in
his honor. All of these varieties of finches are different from

the finches on the mainland of South America. Darwin's finches have changed, i.e. evolved, to become more efficient at obtaining the various types of foods found on the islands. One type of finch evolved a strong beak for cracking seed hulls. One variety evolved to become a sort of woodpecker. You could say that the species split and evolved to fill all empty and available ecological niches. Darwin reasoned that the variety that evolved to become a sort of woodpecker could not have evolved in that direction if there had already been a woodpecker in residence on the islands. A species already evolved to fill an ecological niche will get all the food available in that niche, and another species cannot compete while it evolves in that direction. It is very much like the difference between professionals and rank amateurs in any field.

From Darwin's observations we can make a list of the general requirements for an environment that can produce rapid evolution. The first requirement is that it be rather small. Changes in a species come about by the natural laws of inheritance from some lucky first ones. The larger the population, or the more spread out it is, the longer it takes. The next requirement is isolation. It must be hard to enter or to leave; but it must not only be possible to enter, it must be mandatory, because it is a law of nature that no animal species willingly exchanges an environment to which it is accustomed for any other. We can be sure that the first finches on the Galápagos islands would have gone back to South America if they could have.

Also, the new environment must be somewhat different from the old. For changes in the environment spur evolution. Next there must be some available and empty ecological niches. Finally, the competition for survival should be primarily between the individuals within the evolving species rather than against predators or the forces of nature. These last two tend to hold down, or limit, the size of a population.

But before the "survival of the fittest" can really take effect, the species must overpopulate the environment. Think of the way that cows and sheep can share a pasture, but only because of human supervision. If left to themselves the population of both would expand until there was not enough grass for all. Then the cows would die because the sheep are more efficient at cropping grass. It is the same within an evolving species. Those with some advantage will survive. But those without the advantage will not vanish unless the environment is overpopulated. Fortunately for evolution, every species without efficient predators will quickly multiply to overpopulate any environment, no matter how large.

Let's summarize Darwin's general requirements for a place that will produce rapid evolution: Such a place will be isolated, rather small, have some differences, and one or more available ecological niches. To these general requirements we can add some specific requirements for the hypothetical place where our species was born. The first is that this place should be in or near Africa. Why? Because Proconsul lived in Africa, and while some species of animals migrate a long way, this is not true of the apes. They do not move more than they must. Modern humans may have some degree of wanderlust. But if so, this is an attribute that our species picked up after our lines split. As we know, Ramapithecus spread out all over the world, but Ramapithecus came millions of years after Proconsul.

We can presume that the differences in environments encountered by our apelike ancestors would be differences that would tend to change our ancestors from apes into men. Keeping in mind that nature is seldom subtle, we should be able to deduce what these differences in environment were. For example, Proconsul was acclimated for an arboreal existence. No animal will willingly change environments. But humans do not live in trees now. So we must assume that our ancestors lived for a very long time in a place where there were no trees, or at least not enough trees to make continual dependence on trees possible.

One of the most obvious differences between men and chimpanzees is that humans have very little body hair and chimpanzees have a lot. Recalling Dollo's law, a species does not lose a feature just because a change in the environment makes a feature useless. The environmental change must make the feature a handicap before evolution will remove it. It is not hard to think of a reason or environmental condition where body hair is a handicap. All around the world the animals that live in cold places have a lot of hair. As the climates get hotter, the animals have progressively less hair. Humans are not exactly naked apes, but for the amount of body hair we have, we might as well be. There is only one simple explanation for our hairless bodies. Our ancestors spent a long time in some very hot place. A place even hotter than Africa, where our cousins, the chimpanzees, never found it advantageous to shed their fur coats.

It is always nice when a deduction is supported by independent collaborating evidence. There is evidence galore that our species spent a long time in a hot place. This evidence is inside us, but we do not have to dissect a human to find it. All we need to do is look at a human who is hot. You will see the sweat running off him or her.

But no one will ever see sweat pouring off a chimpanzee or any other ape. They simply do not have the equipment. Compared to our species all apes have extremely few sweat glands. As a result, humans can tolerate much higher temperatures than any ape. The sauna baths that we enjoy would quickly kill a chimpanzee—or almost any other animal for that matter. Features such as sweat glands do not evolve by accident. Only useful features evolve.

It should go almost without saying that the heat encountered by our ancestors was dry heat. When both the temperature and humidity are high, it does no good to sweat, and humans cannot endure moist heat any better than any other animal. So we can presume that our birthplace was both hot and dry. This automatically explains why there were few trees there, because most trees require a lot of water. Furthermore, trees give off moisture that raises the humidity.

When an animal sweats, the water comes out of the blood.

There is salt in the blood. If only water were extracted from the blood, the salt ion concentration would rise and become fatal. So when an animal sweats, salt is excreted with the sweat. Later, when fresh water is added to the system, the salt ion concentration may be too low, so it is necessary to add salt. This is very important when humans sweat a lot. Today we take an abundance of salt for granted, but wars have been fought to insure supplies of salt for a nation. Taxes on salt have led to rebellions as recently as this century. So in the hot, dry place where our ancestors evolved, we must assume there was a good bit of salt available.

We have now assembled a pretty good picture of the place where our ancestors evolved. We can get out our maps, and if such a place exists, we should be able to recognize it. The hot, dry requirements suggest a desert. Africa has many deserts. But deserts get cold at night. Furthermore, deserts lack the necessary isolation. The Afar triangle area in northern Ethiopia looks pretty good, but this area is too new to be considered. It was at the bottom of the Red Sea until fairly recent times. In fact, there is no place in Africa that comes near to meeting the requirements for our birthplace.

Leaving Africa, we come to the area around the Dead Sea. This area meets most of the requirements. The Dead Sea is really a large salt lake, so there is plenty of salt. The large body of water insures a fairly constant temperature. The surface of the Dead Sea is 1,289 feet below the level of the Mediterranean, so the constant temperature is hot. Summertime temperatures approach 140°F., and in the winter the thermometer seldom registers below 80°F. No animal needs a fur coat there.

Yet despite the high temperatures, the air is so dry that the heat can be tolerated. In fact, this area has been called a "land of milk and honey." However, this region lacks the isolation necessary to have been our birthplace. The geological history of this place proves that this lack of isolation has always been the case—at least during the time of interest to us.

If we wished, we could continue searching worldwide for a place that meets all the requirements for our birthplace, but we would search in vain. There is absolutely no place on earth that meets all these requirements.

Well now! What does this mean? Is it possible that Darwin was wrong after all? Could our very own bodies be lying to us about the place where some of our special features evolved? The answer to both these last questions is no. True, there is no place on earth now that meets the requirements for our birthplace. But then there is now no land bridge between America and Asia either. This old world has changed around considerably from time to time. We have searched the world for our birthplace only in modern space. We have not searched the world in time. So let's look at the history of the world itself.

Why should the world's surface move around? The answer to this question was not firmly answered until the early 1960s. Then it was proven that the crust of the world is not all in one piece like the skin of an apple. Instead it is composed of a number of chunks called "tectonic plates," all floating like rafts on the molten interior of the world. Incidentally, this interior is kept hot enough to be molten by the decay of radioactive elements. (We live on an atomic heat plant.) Currents in the liquid inside of the world cause the plates to move. When plates rub, earthquakes result.

When the India plate slammed into the Asia plate, the Himalaya Mountains were pushed up. Also, the leading edge of the India plate slid under the Asia plate. That's why the Himalayas are so high. The earth's crust under them is two plates thick. (If you would like to know more about this subject, read *Continents Adrift and Continents Aground,* a collection of articles from *Scientific American,* published in book form by W. H. Freeman, 1976.)

About two hundred million years ago, all of the continents were pushed together into a supercontinent we call Pangaea also known as Gondwana Land. South America broke from Africa and drifted away. It is still drifting farther away, at about one inch per year. North America broke from Europe and drifted away, forming the North Atlantic Ocean. The Mediterranean Sea is the water-filled crack between the Africa plate and the Europe/Asia plate. It has changed size and shape considerably from time to time in the past.

All of these earth movements played important parts in the evolution of animals. When South America and Africa were joined, they were considerably farther south than they are now. The ice ages of the time covered these lands with glaciers, but the rest of the world was ice free. As the continents moved north, the changing climates caused the animals to evolve in response to the changes in their environments. But by about sixty-five million years ago, this earth had settled down to very much its present configuration. With few further changes in environment, there were few further changes in the animals.

The ice ages continued to come and go. The ice ages lasted thousands of years, too. But the few score thousand years of an ice age is too brief a period to have much effect on the evolution of any species that lives in a normal environment. Evolution is slow!

Much of the data on the movements of the continents came from the efforts of exploration and survey ships like the *Glomar Challenger.** The chief research tool of this ship is a drill, like the drills used to dig oil wells. The drill of the *Glomar Challenger,* however, is hollow. It is used in deep water, and long columns of the material drilled through, called cores, can be brought up for study. The beds of the seas are not barren rock. There is a constant rain of fish bones and other debris that blankets the sea bottom. This blanket builds up at the rate of a few inches per century. Much of the material in this blanket consists of microscopic sea shells. These creatures have their preferential water temperatures, so a change in the types of shells means a change in the water tempera-

---

*The *Glomar Challenger* is operated by the Scripps Institution of Oceanography.

ture at some time in the past. The ice ages show up clearly in the layers of the shells in the cores. This permits the cores to be used as calendars. Layers of volcanic ash in the cores can be dated.

One of the things that the *Glomar Challenger* and the other exploration ships discovered is that the bed of the Atlantic Ocean has been under water ever since the ocean was formed. In turn, this means there never was an Atlantis. At least there never was an Atlantis in the Atlantic where Plato located this island and city.

Plato's books *Timaeus* and *Critias* are our only sources for the legend of Atlantis. In these books, Plato said that the story was told by Egyptian priests to a Greek visitor named Solon. The priests described the city of Atlantis and set the date of its destruction as nine thousand years past.

Plato's contemporaries said the story of Atlantis was fiction; so have most educated persons since. And yet recent discoveries indicate there might have been some truth to the story. In *A Voyage to Atlantis* by James W. Mavor (Souvenir Press of Great Britain, 1969), the author points out that there has always been trouble with the decimal points in ancient Greek and Egyptian numerals, so that 100 might easily be translated as 1,000.

With this in mind, it is pointed out that there is a small Greek island, now known as Thera, which was destroyed by a volcano in the year 1500 B.C., as nearly as we can determine. Excavations on Thera show that the city that once existed there—if all of Plato's dimensions for Atlantis are divided by ten—fits the description of Atlantis very well. Even the date fits if adjusted in this way. Solon was a real person, and he visited Egypt in 590 B.C. If the nine thousand years were really nine hundred, adding the dates gives 1490 B.C. as the date of the destruction of Atlantis. Nonetheless, Thera was never the head of an ancient civilization. It was only a tiny part of the empire of Crete.

In 1970, the *Glomar Challenger* entered the Mediterranean on a rather short and routine trip. The scientists aboard her did not really expect to find anything unusual, but they did. They made two fairly important discoveries—by accident. One they reported; one they overlooked.

Before we relate what the *Glomar Challenger* found and what it missed, a short description of the Mediterranean Sea is in order. The sea is 2,820 miles long east to west and up to 1,080 miles across north to south. It covers 1,145,000 square miles, making it four and a quarter times the size of Texas. As might be expected of a crack in the earth's crust, the Mediterranean is also quite deep. The edges fall off sharply, and the bottom is two to two and a half miles down in some places. The only natural connection of the Mediterranean with the oceans is through the Strait of Gibraltar. The Strait is only eight and a half miles wide and barely a thousand feet deep.

A lot of water evaporates from the Mediterranean Sea and much of this evaporation falls as rain on the surrounding land. But the greater part of the water that evaporates is blown so far by the winds that it never finds its way back to the sea. More water is permanently lost to the sea in this way than is brought in by all of the rivers. As a result, there is a constant net inflow of salty Atlantic Ocean water through the Strait of Gibraltar. Between two and three cubic miles of water per day are required to make up the losses through evaporation. When water evaporates, the salt is left behind. Therefore the Mediterranean Sea is much saltier than the Atlantic and is getting saltier every day.

All of the above, and more, was known about the Mediterranean by the crew of the *Glomar Challenger* back in 1970. As mentioned earlier, they did not expect to find any surprises. Still, they were more than mildly interested to note that their sonic depth-finder was giving some rather unusual readings.

Sonic depth-finders are used on most ships. These devices create a supersonic "ping" that is directed at the sea bottom. The sound wave hits the bottom and is reflected back up as an echo. The water depth is obtained by recording the time it takes the sound wave to make the round trip. All over the

Mediterranean the sonic depth-finder of the *Glomar Challenger* was not getting just one echo from the bottom per ping, it was getting two. It seemed as though part of each sound wave was bouncing up from the bottom, as expected, and a part was penetrating the bottom to be reflected upward from a second bottom, far below the first.

The scientists of the *Glomar Challenger* were not surprised by the double echoes. These had been reported before—in 1961—by the crew of the exploration ship *Globe*. Further investigation of this phenomenon was one of the reasons for the 1970 trip of the *Glomar Challenger*. The *Glomar Challenger* crew picked out some places to investigate. They let down their drill and drilled down to and through the lower bottom of the Mediterranean Sea. They lifted the drill cores up to the deck. They found, as expected, that the lower bottom of the Mediterranean is a tremendously thick layer of salt—up to a mile thick—and under two miles of water.

The experts on the *Glomar Challenger* concluded that in the fairly recent past, the Strait of Gibraltar was closed by a relatively minor earth movement. Then as now, there was more water permanently lost by evaporation than was brought in by all the rivers—so the Mediterranean Sea dried up. Later the dam at the Strait broke, and the Atantic Ocean refilled the Mediterranean basin. In the meantime, though, so much dirt and sand was blown into the basin that the salt became buried too deep for the water to reach and melt it when the sea refilled.

The oceanographers on the *Glomar Challenger* completed their chores and dated their cores. The top layer on the bed of the Mediterranean is a layer of marine sediment. Dating this material is the specialty of such scientists. They determined that the Mediterranean Sea refilled just about five and a half million years ago.

Under the marine sediment and above the salt is a layer of dirt and sand. Dating layers of windblown material is not the specialty of the crew of the *Glomar Challenger*. It is not the specialty of anyone. The dating must be obtained by indirect methods.

There have always been problems with the dating of ancient events. Even radiometric dating methods are not always to be trusted. To get around this difficulty, as you may be aware, scientists use a relative time calendar that shows the order in which some events took place. But it does not show how long they took or how far back they were. The calendar used today is essentially the same one as that invented by Mr. William Smith near the end of the eighteenth century.

Darwin used this calendar and tried to put some dates in it and ran into trouble. Darwin had been educated as a minister and knew that the church had established, from the "begats" in Genesis, that the world was created on October 28, 4004 B.C. Darwin also knew that this did not allow nearly enough time for human evolution to take place, so he consulted the leading scientists of his time and was told that the world could not possibly be older than ten million years. That was still not nearly enough time for the evolution of the species. Darwin worried about contradicting both the church and the scientists, but finally he went ahead and published his theories anyway.

Some dates have been inserted in the calendar of ancient events, but as mentioned in Chapter One, the scientists in one field do not pay much attention to the work of scientists in another. For example, the dates in the calendars used in different fields do not agree. When did Africa bump into Europe? Geologists say it was just a few million years ago, though paleontologists say they have the bones of the same species of animals, from both Africa and Europe, which are proof of a much earlier closing. The point of all this is: Don't take any ancient dates too seriously, perhaps not even the ones given in this book.

We will, nonetheless, try to establish a date. When Africa moved north and slammed into Europe, at the terrific velocity of about one inch per year, the eastern end of the Mediterranean Sea was closed. We will not try to date this event. After the continents bumped, though, Africa continued to push against Europe. Something had to give. It did. The Great Rift Valley was formed.

The Great Rift Valley, the encyclopedias say, was caused by the relieving of tension stresses in the earth's crust. The crust ripped apart, in two roughly parallel lines, and the earth between these rips fell—in some places as much as a mile. The valley starts in Syria. The Jordan River flows down it. The Dead Sea is within it. The valley follows the Red Sea to Africa. Some say the formation of the valley also created the Red Sea. Some say the rifting merely followed an existing weak crack in the bed of the Red Sea. No matter, the marine deposits on the floor of the Red Sea indicate that the seabed cracked open about twenty million years ago. The Great Rift Valley extends from the southern end of the Red Sea southward across Africa to Mozambique, and probably farther.

All earth movements are caused by the relief of stresses in the tectonic plates of the earth. When the Strait of Gibraltar was closed, though, stresses were not relieved in that vicinity. Stresses were created. Compressive stresses. These could have been the result of the relief of much greater tensional stresses elsewhere, and the only record we have of major tensional stress relief in that general time frame is the Great Rift Valley. It does not seem unreasonable to assume that the two events were related and occurred about the same time.

Back to the *Glomar Challenger*. As mentioned earlier, the scientists were not surprised at finding a salt layer under the seabed. However, they were very excited about one of the implications of their discovery. Oil is frequently found under the salt layers that are formed when a sea dries up. There are salt layers under the bed of the Gulf of Mexico, for example, and drilling towers have been constructed far out at sea to get at the oil under the salt. The monetary value of oil may have been the reason the scientists of the *Glomar Challenger* apparently overlooked another implication of their discovery. So we will look into it for them, leaving the fields of evolution, taxonomy, plate tectonics, geology, and oceanography for another branch of science—the science of meteorology.

CHAPTER 4

WHERE WE BEGAN

APPROXIMATELY TWENTY MILLION years ago the Strait of Gibraltar was closed by a relatively minor earth movement. Then as now, more water was permanently lost through evaporation than was brought in by all of the rivers. Therefore the Mediterranean Sea dried up. There is no question that it happened. The technical reports of the *Glomar Challenger* for 1970 are a matter of public record. However, there may be some questions as to how that event affected the evolution of humans. This chapter will answer those questions.

There is no need to guess about what events took place as the Mediterranean Sea dried up. These events followed natural laws so we can report those events just as though we were eyewitnesses. The first thing that happened, of course, is that the sea level fell. This caused the surface area to shrink. Since the rate of evaporation is proportional to surface area, the rate of evaporation slowed down. This meant there was progressively less and less rain to fall on the surrounding lands. A drought began, which became worse and worse. There is, by the way, geological evidence for this drought.

As the level of the Mediterranean fell, the waters became saltier. All marine life died. Later the waters became supersaturated with salt, and the excess began dropping out as a rain onto the bottom of the sea. As the water shrank away from the banks, this salt layer was exposed as a glistening white border. The border became wider and wider, forming a salt desert that extended around the sea.

The waters of the Mediterranean divided and formed into brine lakes that lay in the deepest parts of the seabed. These salt lakes did not completely dry up, of course. They were kept liquid by the waters from the rivers that continued to run and emptied into the Mediterranean.

Let me digress to state that not all of the rivers emptying into the Mediterranean are totally dependent on rain that originates with water evaporated from the Mediterranean Sea. The Nile River gets most of its water from rain that evaporated out of the Indian Ocean. The Rhone and Po Rivers are also fairly independent of Mediterranean water for their volume. The Volga and the Danube may or may not have had outlets to the Mediterranean at that time. No matter; it is sufficient that some rivers continued to flow during the drought.

Except for the salt lakes at the end of each of the rivers, the bottom of the basin was covered with a terrifically thick bed of salt. Nothing could live there. The salt desert did not last long, however. As the drought on the mainland killed the plants, the soil was free to move. Billions of tons of soil were moved by the winds. Even today places as far away as England are bothered by dust blown from North Africa. Then as now, a lot of the windblown dust, dirt, and sand dropped into the Mediterranean. The salt deserts vanished, but they were replaced by conventional deserts, although these deserts were hotter and drier than anything we can compare them with today.

All this paints a bleak picture of the dried-up Mediterranean. But there were mitigating forces at work. Today the Mediterranean area is considered semitropical. However, the mild climate is due to the large body of water, rather than its latitude. Take away the water and the climate would be considerably cooler, because the Mediterranean is fairly far north. Naples and New York City are at the same latitude. The lower edge of the Mediterranean is even with Austin, Texas, the upper edge with Minneapolis, and there is a lot of cold weather between those cities. At the bottom of the basin it was hot, true, but not as hot as a direct comparison with temperatures around the Dead Sea might indicate.

Just how hot was it down there? We cannot be sure; we cannot even estimate. Going down in deep mines the temperatures rise about 30°C (54°F) per mile, but we cannot use their figures directly. The heat in mines is held in by the mine shafts. The hot air at the bottom of the Mediterranean basin could, and did, get blown away and mixed up with cooler air by the prevailing winds. Still, there is no argument about the fact that it was hot.

The Mediterranean basin would have been totally uninhabitable except for one thing: There was rain that fell within the basin. To account for this rain, step halfway around the world and take a look at the western coast of Australia. This area has one of the heaviest rainfalls of anywhere in the world. The prevailing winds are from the west. As these winds cross the seas, they pick up a lot of moisture. There is a mountain range on the west coast of Australia. When the winds hit these mountains, they are diverted upward. The rising air cools, and the moisture condenses out as rain. But nearly all of this rain falls on the western slopes of the mountains. On the eastern side of the mountains is a desert that is one of the driest places in the world.

The same meteorological system was working in the Mediterranean basin. Clouds formed over the shrinking sea, and the winds blew these clouds away. At first the rising slopes of the old seashore presented no obstacle. But when the Mediterranean Sea got to be a few hundred feet below present sea level, the winds and clouds were diverted upward. The clouds cooled and turned into rain. Rain fell inside the old sea basin to wet the windblown soil and form eventually into streams that found their way down into the depths to the salt lakes. When this runback plus the water from the rivers equaled the amount of water permanently lost by evaporation, the salt lakes stopped shrinking. Please note that the deeper down the salt lakes were, the more efficiently this system worked.

Where there is rainwater, there is life. Plant seeds blown in by the winds, along with the dirt, sprouted and grew. Vast pastures came into being on the sloping sides of the Mediterranean basin. Other pastures formed on the upwind sides of the mountains that had once been islands. Skimpy pastures, perhaps, but a lot more habitable than the deserts that had existed before. Animal life did not move into these pastures. Animals were stopped by the terrible deserts that commenced just over the rim of the old seashore. Also, these pastures were too hot to be attractive to the grass-eating animals if they had a choice.

The watered areas in the basin of the Mediterranean can be compared to the miniature gardens called terrariums, which we can grow in bottles. Within the bottles, any moisture that evaporates will condense on the sides of the bottle. Then the water runs down into the bottom of the bottle to be picked up by the plants and used over and over again. This continuous recycling of the water enables us to avoid having to add makeup water to the gardens for months and even years. The same recycling in the Mediterranean basin allowed even small rivers to maintain quite large habitable areas. These areas deserve a name, and since the discoverer of a new place generally gets to name it, I will call these habitable areas terrariums. There was a Nile terrarium, a Po terrarium, a Rhone terrarium, and others. Even intermittent rivers could have created some small terrariums.

Next, we must show how the terrariums became populated, keeping in mind that animals will not willingly change environments. First a casual glance at a chart of the Mediterranean shows that its banks fall off rather sharply. This means the sea had to drop a considerable distance before the surface area shrank very much. In turn, this means the drought started very slowly. For a long time after the Straits closed, there was very little change in the amount of rainfall on the surrounding lands. But the Mediterranean did not have to drop very far at all to have a profound effect on the rivers.

As the sea fell below the mouth of the rivers, a drop-off formed. This caused the rivers to run faster. The rapidly running waters cut away at the beds of the rivers. Soon the rivers were running on beds of bedrock. Rock does not yield easily to water, so at this time the rivers started cutting away at their banks. The rivers became wider and shallower. Here and there along each river, spray from some little rapids or falls watered the banks. Grass seeds blown in by the winds sprouted. Tree seeds also sprouted and grew, near the water's edge.

You may be wondering about tree seeds. Most of them are too heavy to fly well. But many trees have evolved to have seeds that will pass unharmed through the digestive tract of a bird or animal. Apple seeds, for example. Indeed, such a trip may even be necessary; at least the Italian farmers think so. They feed ripe olives to their chickens and turkeys and recover the seeds before they will plant them to grow new olive trees.

Let's concentrate our attention on the mouths of the rivers, the Nile in particular. As the sea continued to drop, the wide and shallow river formed a waterfall, which plunged into the depths below. Waterfalls produce a lot of spray. Victoria Falls on the Zambezi River can be used as an illustration, although this river is a lot smaller than the Nile. Victoria Falls is 5,580 feet wide and only about 400 feet high. However, the spray from these falls has created and maintained a gigantic rain forest.

A similar rain forest came into being at the mouth of the Nile. It extended for many miles upstream of the falls and spilled over into the basin itself, growing on the remains of the old river delta after the spray had washed out the residual salt. Grass will grow where there is not enough water for trees, so the rain forest was bordered by a wide belt of grass. As the Mediterranean continued to shrink downward, this rain forest grew downward with it, watered by the spray from lower falls and rapids. The forest eventually grew until its lower edge was well over a hundred miles from the mainland and about a mile and a half below.

As the rain forest was forming around the waterfall at the end of the Nile, the flora and fauna of the mainland were beginning to feel the pinch of the ever-increasing drought. Animals dependent on trees, when they could, transferred over to this new rain forest. Those that could not died with their trees. They either starved to death or were killed by the meat-eating predators. Even though the drought started very slowly, evolution is much slower. Tree dwellers did not have nearly enough time to re-evolve to life on the ground. Anyway, the ecological niches for ground dwellers were already occupied. A displaced species cannot possibly evolve to fill an occupied ecological niche without the help of magic. But magic is not needed here. One band of Proconsul's children was able to move into the newly formed rain forest, either as the rain forest grew to merge with others or by coming down the belt of trees that bordered the river.

You may be certain that the native predators found and entered the new rain forest and the surrounding grasslands, too. However, predators have a good bit of freedom of choice over their movements. When the predators prowled down below the rim of the Mediterranean basin, they encountered rising temperatures that made them reluctant to go very far down. However, the tree dwellers did not have any choice. As all animals will, they promptly overpopulated their environment and had to go as far down as there were trees, or starve. Even at that, it is probable that many starved.

The conditions described above did not last very long. Just a few thousand years at the most. Even rock will not hold up forever under rushing water. At the foot of the waterfall, the waters undercut the face of the falls. The face caved in. The debris was washed away, and the falls reformed, but now they were a few feet farther upstream. All waterfalls "walk" upstream in this way. Niagara Falls, for example, has moved through seven miles of rock in the last ten or twelve thousand years.

As the waterfall at the mouth of the Nile moved upstream, it left behind a deep gorge with rock walls. These rock walls choked off the spray. The rain forest at the rim of the basin slowly withered and died. The part of the rain forest up on the mainland moved upstream with the falls, although somewhat reduced in size. The part of the rain forest down in the depths continued to flourish though, since it was watered by the spray from the lower falls and rapids. But a gap in the forest formed at the rim of the basin, and the gap continued to grow. The predators who could pass freely back and forth over the gap elected to stay on the mainland when the gap became too wide to be traveled easily. The lower forest was too hot for them.

The forest people in the lower part of the forest had no such choice. They had to stay with their trees as the gap widened. So did the grass-eaters who lived in the grasslands that bordered the dwindling patch of trees.

Let's digress a bit. As you probably know, the Egyptians built a dam across the Nile River, at Aswan, about seven hundred miles upstream from the Mediterranean. In 1961, before they built this dam, they drilled a series of holes into the riverbed all the way across and extracted cores, as was later done in the *Glomar Challenger*. The Egyptians were somewhat surprised to find an old riverbed, gouged out of solid granite, far below the present riverbed. They correctly deduced that this gorge is what was left behind by a waterfall that had moved upstream from the Mediterranean, at some time in the past when the Mediterranean Sea dried up.

Waterfalls inevitably get lower as they move upstream. And yet at Aswan the falls were still about twice as high as Victoria Falls, so the original falls at the mouth of the river must have been truly tremendous. Incidentally, the Egyptians found saltwater seashells in the cores. This enabled them to make a try at dating the time that the Mediterranean reflooded. They came up with a figure very close to five and a half million years ago.*

Let's go back to the shrinking patch of trees, far down in-

---

*See *Time*, Jan. 26, 1976, pp. 44–45.

side the Mediterranean basin. Eventually erosion tamed the lower stretches of the river, and the spray ceased to be adequate to support any trees. The trees died. Then and only then did the tree dwellers come to the ground and find an environment in which they could survive. By this time the grass-eaters had moved into the forming terrariums. Our ancestors followed them.

If we review the conditions existing at this time in the terrariums, we can see that they met the requirements for a place with rapid evolution. The environment was new and different in many respects from anything ever encountered before. The terrariums were certainly isolated. They were surrounded by many miles of terrible deserts. The terrariums were rather large, but much smaller than a continent. The meat-eaters, who had a choice, were hundreds of miles away on the mainland. That left two ecological niches unoccupied. The niches for scavenger and predator. Our ancestors evolved to fill both these niches, with no competition except from each other.

It is significant to note that fossil animal bones were found on many Mediterranean islands, some many years ago, giving rise to speculations that, at one time in the past, the sea was surely dry. H. G. Wells, in his *Outline of History,* made mention of this over fifty years ago. However, even if the sea were dry, it was a puzzle to account for the animals, because it was well known even then that animals will not willingly change environments. Now, of course, we know that the animals were forced down into the terrariums and later climbed the mountains that are now islands.

The fossil bones on the various islands tell us what types of animals were available to our ancestors in the terrariums. For some specifics, dwarf elephant bones and dwarf hippopotamus bones have been found on Malta, Sicily, Crete, and Cyprus. These have been used as illustrations of parallel evolution. It seems, however, more logical to conclude that the dwarfism took place in the terrariums before the islands were islands. Fossil zebra and rhinoceros bones have been found on Samos and elsewhere, along with dozens of varieties of antelope. Ancient goat and sheep bones are fairly common.

We just might be able to clear up one of the puzzles of mythology. Ulysses, you may recall, reported finding sheep as big as modern cows on one of the Mediterranean islands. Sailors are not always truthful, but sheep that big really did live in Africa up until a couple of million years ago. A flock that had been forced down into the terrariums might have been able to climb a mountain to persist to near historic times.

Before we leave this chapter, we should point out that certain events in the past may not have taken place exactly as related. For example, there is strong evidence that for a considerable time there was not just one Mediterranean Sea, but two, divided by a land bridge between Africa and Italy. However, salt beds have been found under both ends of the sea, so both ends became isolated and dried up. Still, one end may have dried up well before the other.

At first the terrariums may have been confined to one end of the basin. The land bridge, if there was one, probably vanished due to the rising, sinking, and tilting of the raftlike tectonic plates under the Mediterranean, caused by the removal and subsequent readdition of the weight of the million cubic miles of water inside the sea. Along these lines it is pertinent to point out that when the sea was dry, the plates were unloaded and, hence, the sea bottom may not have been as far down as it is now. It will be nice when further discoveries clear these points up; but regardless, this outline of our prehistory should not be affected much.

CHAPTER 5

CREATION OF HUMANS, PHASE I

O UR DIRECT LINE of ancestors lived in the terrariums for fifteen million years, give or take a few million. The environment of those places reshaped their bodies inside and out. The term "environment," it must be noted, includes the social as well as physical environment. Both had their effects on our species.

The first requirement for the survival of any species is a food supply. When the moving highway of trees that had brought our ancestors to the terrariums vanished, our ancestors lost their preferential foods. But there was another food available: meat. It is significant that raw meat contains virtually everything necessary to maintain life. True, modern people do sometimes get scurvy from a meat diet, but that meat is cooked meat. The cooking destroys vitamins naturally present in raw meat. Our remote ancestors ate raw meat obtained from the bodies of the grass-eaters. Without efficient predators, these grass-eaters soon overpopulated their environment. The continual near-starvation of all brought about a short life span to all. Our ancestors followed the herds of grass-eaters, not as predators, not at first anyway, but as scavengers.

By necessity, not by choice, our ancestors shifted from an essentially vegetarian diet to an essentially all-meat diet. This change in diet brought about a change in their body shape. Vegetable foods do not have the energy found in meat, and what energy there is, is harder to extract. Consequently, vegetarian animals have relatively long guts. This accounts for the "potbelly" on chimpanzees and gorillas. Meat-eaters have relatively short guts, as an unnecessary length of intestine is a handicap. The intestines of our ancestors shortened somewhat to give modern humans the slim-waisted shape so admired today.

Without efficient predators, our ancestors also multiplied to overpopulate their food supply. It was inevitable that different bands of scavengers would meet at the carcass of some grass-eater. When this happened, the bands fought. One of the bands would be driven off. Those that could not leave were added to the larder of the victors. Meat is meat. All animals physically capable of cannibalism are cannibalistic when necessary for survival. Rats eat rats. Lions eat lions. Dogs eat dogs. Yes, and even modern, civilized humans will eat humans rather than starve. (Read *Survive!*, by Clay Blair, Jr., [Berkley, 1973], for an example. This book describes how the survivors of a 1972 airplane crash were able to stay alive by eating the bodies of those who died in the crash.)

The first settlers in the terrariums were not good hunters. They were just not built right to be hunters. Hunting also requires some instinctive skills, which take an extremely long time to evolve. These first settlers could do little to keep the population of the grass-eaters down. Like modern baboons, they could probably catch a newborn fawn on occasion or finish off an old bull almost dead anyway, but they could neither catch nor kill the healthy adult grass-eaters.

There was one animal species, however, that they could catch and kill: their own. The clashes of different bands at the carcasses of grass-eaters were frequent but not very profitable. It did not take them long to find out that such clashes were to be avoided unless their side had a big advantage. However, lone individuals could be acquired by even a small band without too much danger or trouble. Lone individuals did not last long. The species acquired the instinct to never be alone, an instinct still present in us today. This is one of the reasons solitary confinement is such a dreaded punishment and why we form clubs and social groups.

The smaller bands could not compete with the larger bands in the scavenging of the herds of grass-eaters. But the small bands could scavenge the large bands. A child who strayed too far would be snapped up. A female who lagged behind her band to give birth would find strangers, more hungry than helpful, between her and her group. Over the ages our ancestors acquired hunting skills from practicing on each other.

After a million years or so of such existence, even those dumb animal ancestors of ours came to realize that other bands were enemies. Large bands would chase smaller bands away, picking up all stragglers as they lagged behind. The ones that fled and survived were able to survive only by fleeing so far into the deserts that the pursuers, who had a choice, were unwilling to keep up the chase. Some of these refugees got lost and later found and populated the other terrariums. There history repeated itself. But as each terrarium was somewhat different from all others, further evolution was not exactly parallel.

It was extremely hard to get out of the terrariums. However, one band eventually made it to the outside world. There they found the living fairly easy. Their many years of constant combat with their cousins had caused them to evolve to such an extent that they were more than capable of survival. They could hunt and kill some of the smaller animals. They could avoid the predators. There was vegetable food in abundance. So to celebrate, these refugees multiplied and spread out all over the earth.

We have found relics of these creatures in France, China, India, and in Africa. We call them Ramapithecus. They were not our ancestors. However, they may be considered a sample of a stage of development that our ancestors rapidly passed through. But as far as the Ramapithecine are concerned, when they left the terrariums for the outside world, they left a place of rapid evolution for a place with slow evolution. Spontaneous changes continued to show up in some individuals, of course, but a beneficial change in a creature in China would take a frightfully long time to spread to the ones in France.

Contrast this with the mechanics of evolution down in one of the terrariums. In an environment of only a few hundred square miles, any chance genetic advantage soon became common to the entire population, especially when the advantage was used to eliminate those without that lucky genetic accident.

How fast did those remote ancestors of ours breed? We do not know. But we can be certain that, like all animals, they bred as fast as they could. We can use what we know about modern humans to make a rough estimate. Since about the year 1600, the population of the world has increased at a remarkably steady rate of 2 percent per year. This does not sound like much, but if this rate continues for just one thousand years, the year 2600 will see 980,000,000 persons for each loving couple back in 1600. The fifteen thousand thousand years our ancestors spent in the terrariums were times of continual overpopulation problems. However, a group that got out had no particular problem in filling up the earth.

Refugees from other terrariums made it to the outside world from time to time. Since evolution took a slightly different path in each terrarium, we now have the relics of a host of ancient apelike men, or manlike apes, that seem to have suddenly appeared without having had direct ancestors, persisted awhile without much, if any, further evolution, and then became extinct. I still see no need to list these creatures or describe them. They were not our ancestors.

Let's return to the terrariums. There were no trees. Our ancestors lived on the ground. This in itself does not account for the upright stance of modern people, but we can solve the mystery with what we now know of the environment. First, though, let's take a look at modern baboons. They have been essentially ground dwellers for millions of years and yet show few signs of turning into creatures that walk erect. This is because, if trees are available, baboons will use them. The handlike hind feet of the baboon is a feature with survival advantage. So this feature will not leave the species.

Our early ancestors in the terrariums also had handlike hind feet. But down there, those feet were not an advantage. They were a handicap. Baboons sometimes stand up on their hind feet to look around, but the points of major interest to a baboon are generally nearby points on the ground. These points are their food: lizards, bugs, berries, etc. Baboon hands needed to be near the ground to be efficient in snatching up anything good to eat before it got away or a brother grabbed it. In the terrariums, the potential food was some grass-eater, in trouble, some distance away. Our ancestors had to keep an eye on the herds. They also had to keep the other eye on other bands of scavengers, who were also, they hoped, some distance away. Those who could spot grass-eaters in trouble the farthest, and other bands the farthest, were the ones who survived. Therefore our species evolved to stand erect.

Let's drop down to the salt lakes at the lowest places in the terrariums. As all animals that sweat a lot must, our ancestors visited these lakes for salt. There they learned to swim. This was quite an accomplishment, because chimpanzees (and presumably Proconsul also) have a dread of getting near ground water that amounts to a phobia. It is believed that this phobia results from the fact that all ground waters in Africa have long been contaminated with crocodiles. Regardless of the reason for the phobia, it exists, and as a result, our zoos can exhibit chimpanzees on small islands rather than behind bars. The chimpanzees cannot force themselves to enter the water that they could easily wade across.

Since our ancestors must be presumed to have had this phobia also, there must have been some compelling reason for them to learn to swim. There was. There was food in the salt lakes. Nothing could live in these briny waters, of course, but every flood down river brought more than mud and trash. The rivers brought in meat. Perhaps half a hippo that slipped over the falls. A crocodile that lost an argument with a brother. Drowned deer. Dead fish.

Fresh flesh will sink in fresh water, but it floats in brine. As the meat entered the salt lakes, it rose to the top. The winds pushed it ashore. Our ancestors feasted. Fortunately, salt is a preservative. At the shoreline, the strongest, not the smartest, got the most meat. Finally, one of the smarter ones figured out that he could get his share if he waded out. Actually, he probably wasn't so smart. He was just too hungry for his instincts to keep him out of the water.

Note that the chimpanzees we exhibit on little islands are well fed. They probably would escape if they were starving. In the salt lakes, those that waded out found they could not sink in those briny waters. They learned to swim. Today our species is virtually free of the phobia about entering water. Why? Because after a few million years, a species that must do something to survive will evolve to have an instinct to enjoy it. There is no other rational reason why otherwise sane persons will put up with the trouble and expense that "a day at the beach" costs them. It must be an instinct.

It should not be necessary to show that the environment of the terrariums caused our species to lose its body hair. It was just too hot down there for them to keep that hair. However, please note that the body hair was lost in the terrariums. This means that it was lost over five million years ago. Any drawings of later prehumans, to be accurate, should show them with no more hair than modern humans.

While we are on the subject of illustrations, those relatively recent prehumans should be shown with the noses of modern humans instead of the apelike noses generally depicted, because our noses evolved in the terrariums, too. Our nasal passages are primarily ways for air to get to our lungs. Our lungs require warm, moist, and dust-free air. In the terrariums, the air was not just warm, it was hot. The air was also very dry and frequently full of dust. Our noses evolved to cool incoming air, moisturize it, and filter out the dust.

Any unbiased analysis of the mechanics of our noses confirms this statement. Before our species left the terrariums, our ancestors all had the large, hooked, eagle-beaked noses of modern desert nomads. The wide diversity of modern nose shapes came much later in response to localized conditions. For example, large noses get frostbitten much easier than small ones. A frostbitten nose is a severe handicap to a hunter and to his family. This is why modern Laplanders and Eskimos have such small noses.

Before going on we must bring up a few more of the facts of evolution. Each change stems from a chance change in the DNA of an individual. These changes, or mutations, are rare because DNA is tough stuff. All mutations are rare, and beneficial mutations are much rarer. Beneficial mutations are so rare today that it is argued that there hasn't been enough time for Proconsul's children to change into us. However, this too has a simple and natural explanation.

First, it has been noted that insects raised in laboratories where the temperatures were high have an abnormally high percentage of mutations. However, we do not know if this applies to humans. So let's skip the high temperatures in the terrariums as a source of change in DNA.

DNA is extremely resistant to change, but it can be changed. Hard radiation will produce mutations. All humans are constantly bombarded with hard radiation, both from the skies above and from the earth below. The terrariums were a few miles closer to the radioactive core of the earth, but this did not necessarily produce many mutations. There was still adequate shielding. Some viruses will produce mutations. For example, measles. Not always, but sometimes. However, it is unlikely that viruses played much part in our evolution. This leaves drugs and poisons as the remaining known things that will alter DNA. (Remember thalidomide?)

Drugs and poisons were available in the terrariums. Many plants have evolved to contain drugs and poisons because, as we might say, plants don't like to be eaten. Our species, like all animal species, evolved a sense of taste to give warning of these noxious substances. They are detected as a "bad" taste. For example, the bitter taste of spinach is the result of our species having evolved to detect the oxalic acid in spinach as something to be avoided.

But starving creatures will override the warnings given by their taste buds and eat literally anything. Clay, grass, leaves, bark, even spinach. All species thrust into a new environment will have a hungry time of it at first, but usually a species will either become extinct or will adapt to the new environment. And predators, or other natural causes, will keep the population down so that the individuals generally get enough to eat.

In the terrariums, the entire population was chronically hungry for fifteen million years. When they could not get meat, they ate plants that no well-fed creature would touch. Many persons, no doubt, died from the vegetable drugs and poisons; however, there were also many that survived near-lethal doses and subsequently had children who were somewhat different. Mutations are rare today, true, but it wasn't always so.

Generally, harmful mutations brought quick death to the unlucky ones that had them, but this was not always so, either. Some mutations affect only recessive genes. They require that both parents have the same recessive gene before the harmful mutation will show up, and even then there is only one chance in four that it will appear. Today our species has over two thousand more or less undesirable genetic conditions tucked away in its genes, every individual possessing several. Many of these are part of the price we paid, and are still paying, for the rapid evolution of our species.

Far more of our uniquely human characteristics were evolved in the terrariums than just those few that we have mentioned here. However, as with our jigsaw puzzle, it seems preferable to press on to get some idea of the overall picture before going into much detail. Later chapters, however, will return us to the terrariums to fill in some of the blanks we are leaving.

CHAPTER 6

HALFWAY THROUGH
THE DESCENT OF MAN

FOR FIFTEEN MILLION YEARS, more or less, our direct line of ancestors lived in the terrariums at the bottom of the dried-up Mediterranean basin. There they evolved to match both the physical and social environment. They evolved to fill the vacant ecological niches of both scavenger and predator.

After so long in an environment conducive to rapid evolution, our ancestors were quite happy down there. The conditions might seem grim to us, but they learned to love their native land, like penguins love the frozen Antarctic. They knew no better. The bodies of our ancestors were modified to prefer that environment, and those modifications are still with our species. Ask any doctor today, "Where is the healthiest place in the world to live?" He will probably refer you to some hot, dry place like Palm Springs, California. My Texas friends tell me that half the population of Texas is composed of people who were given up for dead by eastern doctors. Those persons got into their covered wagons and moved to Texas. *Tejanos* always tell the truth, so this must be so.

All good things must come to an end. Five and a half million years ago our ancestors had to leave their homes and move on. We do not usually know why an animal species changes environments; we only know it is because it must. In this case, however, we do not have to guess. The dam at the Strait of Gibraltar broke.

Please do not imagine that when the dam at the Strait broke, that an immense tidal wave, immediately and irresistibly, swept from one end of the basin to the other like the waves you can make in your bathtub. The opening at the Strait is extremely tiny compared with the vast size of the sea. True, the inrushing Atlantic Ocean water created a spectacular set of falls at the Strait—the *Guinness Book of World Records* (Bantam Books, March 1978) states that these falls were twenty-six times as big as any falls that exist today—but a few hundred miles inland, even turtles, if there were turtles there, could have taken a leisurely departure.

It is not hard to compute how fast the waters rose in the Mediterranean basin. Assuming the Strait immediately opened to its present width of eight and a half miles and its thousand-foot depth (except for a few of the very lowest places), the waters rose at a rate of no more than three feet per day. In the eastern end it was probably less than a foot per day. It took many years for the basin to fill up.

Even though the waters rose slowly in the Mediterranean basin, rise they did. All bottom dwellers had to leave or drown. Our ancestors departed, taking their meager possessions with them, but leaving the bones of their ancestors behind. Incidentally, this clears up one of the big mysteries of anthropology. The mystery of why so few of our ancestors' bones have been discovered.

Some of the bottom dwellers retreated up into the hills. We can forget about them. Some climbed the mountains and later found themselves marooned on islands. Some went up the slopes of the basin and managed to make their way to the outside world.

In Africa, Drs. Dart, Broom, and Leakey have found the bones of two, possibly three, different types of prehumans. Dr. Dart named them the australopithecine. (He later apologized for giving them so long a name. Incidentally, *australo* is from the Latin word for "southern" and *pithecus* is Greek for "ape.")

According to fossil evidence, two, possibly three, types of

part-man, part-ape creatures suddenly appeared in Africa a little under five million years ago. They existed for about three million years and then vanished. Up to now, their sudden appearance has been one of the biggest mysteries of our prehistory. However, we know the solution. These two, possibly three, types of creatures were the descendants of the refugees from two, possibly three, terrariums. The half-million years of lost time need not bother us. Fossils will not form just anywhere. It took those refugees a long time to get to a place where their bones would be preserved to mystify future generations.

The australopithecine were not our ancestors. But they can be considered as a sample, frozen in time, of a state of development our ancestors passed through five and a half million years ago. But when the australopithecine got to Africa, they were more than able to cope. So for them, evolution essentially stopped.

Both varieties of australopithecine were essentially human from the neck down. Indeed, from the jaws down, as their teeth were just about the same as ours. (We don't know enough about the possible third type to try to describe him.) The teeth of Australopithecus *africanus* indicate he was probably a meat-eater, and the teeth of Australopithecus *robustus* hint he was a vegetarian. The relics of these creatures suggest that A. *africanus* may have had A. *robustus* over for dinner fairly often. Incidentally, it is not the shape of the teeth that reveals diet, so much as it is the thickness of the enamel. Meat-eaters have thin enamel. Plant-eaters have thick enamel because the grit in plant food is hard on their teeth.

Perhaps we should digress to clear up the above statement. Plants contain grit because plants, unlike animals, cannot excrete. Everything, except for water and gases, that gets into a plant through its root system, stays inside. Dissolved silica is frequently found in ground waters. The plants cannot use this silica so it is deposited as tiny quartz crystals in the plant cell walls. These very hard crystals will not harm our digestive systems, but they do dull lawn mower blades and wear down teeth. Plant-eaters, in response, have evolved to have either thick tooth enamel or multiple sets of teeth. If you would like some figures, A. *africanus,* as do you and I, had enamel about one millimeter thick on his teeth. A. *robustus* had three millimeters of enamel on his teeth.

The chief difference between the australopithecine and ourselves is in the heads. Their brains were larger than chimpanzee brains, but only one third the size of ours. The terrariums provided our species with our body shapes, but our brain development came later.

Despite their small brains, the australopithecine had more than sufficient intelligence to withstand the forces of nature. We now know that they had no body hair to speak of, so we can be sure that their naked hides were bitten by bugs and scratched by briars. They had lost their ape phobia about ground waters, so they fell victim to crocodiles, malaria, and bilharzia. But they survived for better than three million years, and this is far longer than modern men seem likely to survive. The australopithecine should have been able to make it up to the present day. They would have, too, except for one thing. Remember a few chapters back when we mentioned that two million years ago a number of native African animals suddenly became extinct—a giant pig, a variety of giant sheep, etc. Add Australopithecus to the list of species that suddenly vanished concurrently with the arrival of a new predator, *Homo habilis,* sometimes called the first true man. Any unbiased jury in the world would convict *Homo habilis* of genocide on circumstantial evidence.

Homo habilis preyed on the australopithecine as readily as modern Africans prey on baboons; more readily, in fact, because modern baboons are rather small in size to be considered desirable prey. There used to be some varieties of giant baboons, but they vanished at about the same time Australopithecus entered the area. The bashed-in skulls of these giant baboons are found mixed in with the relics of Australopithecus.

We should not look down our noses at *Homo habilis* because he exterminated the australopithecine. It is a law of nature that two species cannot occupy the same ecological niche in the same environment for very long. One species will eliminate the other, either directly or indirectly.

For example, consider our animal cousins, the chimpanzees and the baboons. If trees are available, the baboons will use them. If, as sometimes happens, chimpanzees are in those trees, the two species are in direct competition within the same ecological niche. If food is plentiful, the two species may seem to coexist peacefully. But actually they do not. According to Jane van Lawick-Goodall, in her book *In the Shadow of Man,* when the two species are near each other, even when the animals are well fed, it is not unusual for a chimpanzee to chase, catch, kill, and eat a baboon youngster. Further, the large baboon male protectors of the troop will not actively oppose the chimpanzees, although they would oppose a leopard or you.

Now you know why baboons spend so much time on the ground. They have been chased out of the trees to the ground where the chimpanzees do not care to go, but the transition to the ground is not complete. Evolution is slow! When *Homo habilis* entered the environment of the australopithecine the two were in direct competition within the same ecological niche, but Australopithecus had nowhere to go where *Homo habilis* would not follow.

(For an example of indirect competition exterminating a species, consider the fate of the saber-toothed tiger who became extinct roughly fifty thousand years ago. Our ancestors of that time were pretty good hunters. *Homo habilis* had started the extermination of the animal species that the saber-toothed tigers needed for food, and by fifty thousand years ago our ancestors had wiped out all of the larger species that could be killed easily. There was no direct conflict between our ancestors and the saber-toothed. Our ancestors wiped out the saber-toothed by doing away with the saber-toothed's food supply.)

The australopithecine, as mentioned before, were not our

direct ancestors. Our ancestors were not among those that made it to the outside world when the Mediterranean basin reflooded. Our direct ancestors were pushed up a large mountain by the rising waters and found themselves marooned on one of the Mediterranean islands.

It is probable that our ancestors, of five and a half million years ago, were members of a species a bit different from any of the known types of Australopithecus. The Mediterranean islands are closer to Europe than Africa, so our direct ancestors probably climbed up out of a terrarium separate from the terrariums that produced A. *Africanus,* A. *robustus,* or the questionable third variety. However, the known varieties were so similar that it is possible that all others were quite similar, too.

The terrariums were a place of rapid evolution. However, the island where our species lived, up to near modern times, was a place of much faster evolution. Our ancestors lived on this island for five million years. They evolved their brains there.

At this time you may be wondering, why hasn't some evidence of millions of years of prehuman residence on some Mediterranean island been discovered? There are at least two answers to this question. One is that it hasn't been looked for. Another is that evidence has been found but not recognized for what it is.

To illustrate these answers, let's leave prehistory and have a scenario. This is a fictive account, but one that could be true. Imagine you are an engineer in charge of some construction on one of the Mediterranean islands. *The island.* One day a workman hands you an old skull bone and remarks that he thinks it is odd that this bone should be so far below ground level. So do you, but you don't say so. Instead you simply say that some old Greek, Roman, or Carthaginian must have been thrown down a well. You put the bone away, and say you'll take care of it. Later in your room that night, you take a close look at the bone. It looks very odd to you. What do you do then? Do you call up the nearest museum or university? Of course not! If you did, a swarm of scientists and government officials would descend on you. Your project would be stopped. But the workmen still have to be paid and the notes on the machinery would have to be met. The contract has a penalty clause. Your superiors would tell you that you were hired to build something, not to play amateur anthropologist. You will be lucky if you are only fired without being blacklisted as well. These things have happened. Engineers know about them. But they will not happen again if the engineers can help it.

If a few hundred gold coins were found, the news might get out. But not the news of the finding of a few old bone scraps, because all the Mediterranean islands are full of old bone scraps. Furthermore, you must keep in mind that, without the skulls, an untrained observer probably could not tell the difference between human bones five million years old and modern human bones. Even among scientists, Dr. Dart had a rough time getting his first Australopithecus skull accepted as anything other than an ape skull, or as the deformed skull of a relatively modern Negro.

There is evidence in existence of prehuman residence of much greater antiquity than credited on a Mediterranean island. But this book is controversial enough. It may well be years before this book is accepted. Then it will be soon enough for someone to take a fresh look at some obscure exhibit in some museum and shout "Eureka!"

CHAPTER 7

CREATION OF HUMANS, PHASE II

F IVE AND A HALF million years ago, give or take a few millenniums, the dam at the Strait of Gibraltar broke, and the Mediterranean Sea reflooded. Our direct line of ancestors was a group who were pushed up a mountainside by the rising waters. Soon they found themselves marooned on an island. On this island our ancestors evolved their intelligence.

How did our ancestors evolve their intelligence? There really should be no mystery about this, but there is. Therefore this chapter will proceed slowly and cover the evolution of intelligence in detail.

Every feature of every species evolved and became common to a species for just one reason. Somehow those features were aids to survival in the environment inhabited by the species at that time. Intelligence—rather, a high degree of intelligence—is a feature of the human species. Somehow the environment inhabited by our species over the last five million years was an environment that favored the survival of the most intelligent and the elimination of all others. It is as simple as that. However, this is only the general reason why our species evolved intelligence. To be more specific, we will need to go on and determine the details of the environment on the island. Not the details of the physical environment; those had little to do with the evolution of intelligence. It was the social environment that produced our brains.

To begin with, think of the trials and tribulations of any

species when forced into a new environment. The species is neither physically nor mentally adapted to cope with the new environment. For example, think of the first of our ancestors that climbed into the trees. Did they climb up for food or to escape predators? We do not know. But we do know two things about these first climbers. They didn't climb trees because they wanted to; they climbed because they had to—and the only alternative was extinction. Also, the first ones to climb trees were not very good at it. This means they had to be very careful about where they placed their feet. They had to think about how they were going to move around.

The ones that could think the best had an advantage. Natural selection favored their survival and eliminated those that either could not or would not abandon the reflexes that had been acquired prior to going up into the trees. This natural selection persisted for thousands of generations.

In general, any species forced to change environments will thereby acquire a higher degree of intelligence. However, this is a self-limiting process. Going back to our first ancestors who climbed up trees, eventually their forms changed to adapt them to life in the trees. They also acquired instincts and reflexes that automatically took care of the decisions necessary for movements.

Today monkeys and apes can travel through the treetops at high speed without having to think about where to place their hands, just as a skilled taxi driver can pilot his cab through traffic without having to think about what he is doing. In both types of activity, reflex actions are better than conscious thought. Reflexes are faster, and delays or hesitations can be fatal.

We can see that, as a species adapts to a new environment, the species acquires reflexes and instincts that are built-in solutions to the problems of survival. Once these inherited solutions to the problems have evolved, there is little or no need for additional intelligence. So the species does not acquire more intelligence. Useless features do not evolve. However, according to Dollo's law, useless features do not vanish from a species either. So the intelligence acquired during a transition period between environments is retained.

We can now see why seals and dolphins are such smart animals. Long ago the ancestors of these species lived on dry land. For some reason that need not concern us, the ancestors of these creatures returned to the sea. In the sea, the land-acquired instincts were worse than useless. The first to return to the sea had to think to stay alive. For thousands of generations, natural selection favored the survival of the best thinkers. Perhaps it still does; however, changes in the physical shapes and the acquisition of new instincts are reducing the value of new advances in intelligence. Seals and dolphins are probably not getting any smarter; however, they are not getting any dumber either.

Now we come to a definition of intelligence. It is the ability to learn and understand from experience and also the ability to respond, quickly and successfully, to a new situation. (This definition comes from *Webster's New World Dictionary*.) Animals can learn by experience to some extent, but when they are confronted with some new situation they do not do so well. The almost universal response to a new situation is to consider it as a threat situation and to respond to it as a threat. *i.e. scientific Creationists*

As far as intelligence is concerned, the first of our ancestors on the island were little more than animals. They had instincts they had acquired in the terrariums, or even farther back. On the island, the instinct-prompted actions were frequently not the optimum course of action.

On the island there were vegetable foods and some animals. However, we must not assume that our ancestors of five million years ago were good hunters. It is probably true, though, that from time to time some hunting skills had appeared in the terrariums. When this happened, a food supply was assured and the human population went up. But the animal species population against which these skills were effective went down. Down to zero. There was only one animal

that our ancestors successfully hunted in the terrariums that
did not become extinct. Their own species. We may be sure
that our ancestors arrived on their island with skills and instincts for hunting each other.

It is the availability of food that governs the size of a band
of animals. There is just so much territory that a band can
cover in the course of a day. If there is not enough food in
this territory to feed the entire band, some must leave or
starve.* We cannot be sure of the size of the bands of the
first arrivals on the island, but since they were little more
than animals, we can be sure that a few generations later they
had overpopulated their island. After that time, the average
size of the bands was necessarily quite small.

In the terrariums, when two bands met at the carcass of a
grass-eater and fought, the losers had a chance to get away if
they could run fast enough because there were always places
to run to. There were the mountains and the deserts. After a
few generations, all living room on the island was occupied.
When two bands met at some food source, perhaps a berry
patch, we can be sure they fought.

The losers who tried to flee, however, would run into the
outstretched arms (and empty bellies) of a neighboring tribe.
Before very long, those with instincts to run away from fights
were extinct. The survivors were those who would stand and
fight, regardless of the odds. This new characteristic made
even very small bands very undesirable prey for any would-be
predators. (As an analogy, think of the Texas Rangers. Those
lawmen had the reputation for being willing to die before re-
treating. As a result, they were seldom called upon to fight
unless there was a mighty good reason.)

Down in the terrariums, our ancestors acquired instincts to
be wary of strangers and to kill strangers if they could. These
instincts still had a lot of survival value on the island, and

---

*There are parts of Texas where, it is said, to get enough to eat, a cow
must graze at twenty miles an hour. Quite naturally you do not see large
herds of cows there.

features with survival value will not leave a species. But at the same time it could be fatal if an individual or a band tried to act on this instinct precipitously. So while the instincts were retained, our ancestors acquired the ability to refrain from acting on these instincts immediately. Those who did not have this ability acted. However, a creature that does act instinctively will be acting in a stereotyped manner. Its actions can be predicted. Those early islanders who could control their instincts were therefore able to eliminate those who could not.

This is where we stand today. Our species has the ability to control or refrain from acting on its instincts. We have not evolved to lose the instincts. Still, many people today deny they have any instincts whatsoever. The idea that there are inherited circuits of nerve cells in our brains that influence our actions is very disturbing to these people. The idea seems to conflict with the concept of free will. It is ironic that those people who most strongly deny that people have instincts are the ones who act the most instinctively. Only those who know of their instincts are able to use logic to control their actions. At the same time, following an instinct is often the best thing to do. After all, every instinct was once the optimum solution to a problem of survival, and many still are. So to clear up any misunderstandings about instincts and how they operate, we will discuss a few prevalent human instincts.

For our first instinct, think of the way most people act when they slip into bed on a cold night. They curl up until the bed gets warm. Why? Well, if you recall your high-school physics, you may remember learning that a warm body loses heat at a rate proportional to the exposed skin surface and that a sphere has the least area relative to volume possible for any shape. When we curl up between cold sheets, we are changing our shapes as much as possible into the shape of a sphere, and this shape is the scientifically best position to assume to conserve body heat. However, we do not have to reason all this out. Humans have the instinct to curl up when they are cold, and the instinct is triggered by the temperature. Even little babies have this instinct. If you see one all sprawled out in its crib like a little frog, it is warm enough. However, if the baby is all huddled up in a ball, it needs more cover.

If you will observe the young of most animal species, you will see another instinct at work. Nearly all the young animals seem to spend an inordinate amount of time and energy in unproductive activity. We call this activity "play." If we think about it, though, we can reason that play is unproductive only in that it does not bring an immediate material gain. The exercise of play is necessary if young muscles are ever to develop their full potential.

However, young animals do not reason. They do not say to themselves, "I must run and jump a lot so that I will grow up big and strong." No, young animals play simply because they have instincts to play. We can classify these instincts as good instincts because they have positive survival value. But, good or bad, why should young animals, or any animals for that matter, follow the prompting of instincts? To get the answer to this question, catch one of the young of our species and ask. "Because I want to; it makes me feel good!" may well be the reply.

There in a nutshell is the reason animals follow their instincts. Each instinct is an inherited arrangement of brain cells that prompts certain actions. These circuits also have connections to pleasure/pain centers in the brain that produce sensations. Doing what an instinct prompts brings pleasant sensations. Not doing what an instinct prompts brings more or less unpleasant sensations. In this particular case, as every parent and teacher knows, the denial of time to play is a dreaded punishment.

What happens when it is impossible for an animal to follow its instincts? Scientists have done a lot of experimentation with animals along these lines, but I have never heard that the experimental animals were improved by the treatment. In fact, it is often fatal to keep animals from following their instincts. It is a tribute to the toughness of the young of our species that they turn out as well as they do after the way we keep them from following their instincts "for their own good." I am not suggesting we stop sending our children to schools where they are forced to sit down and be quiet when their instincts tell them to play. I am merely pointing out that such treatment forces our children to act contrary to their instincts, and such treatment is very hard on animals.

Although most of our children manage to survive, still the incidence of schizophrenia is so high among children that it is often called the young person's disease. Schizophrenia is also described as "a flight from reality." Perhaps it is; however, this so-called reality is a long way removed from the reality of the environment that our species evolved to inhabit.

To continue with this same instinct, most young animals have instincts to play a lot, but the adults of most species do not move around any more than they must. Well, adult muscles need some exercise to keep in shape, but most wild adult animals get far more exercise than they really need just by keeping themselves alive. Unnecessary motions might attract the unwanted attentions of a predator or frighten away potential prey. Unnecessary motions would use up energy that might be needed in an emergency.

There are plenty of good reasons for adult animal inactivity, and most adult animals have instincts that keep them inactive as much as possible. There are exceptions, of course, but our close kin, the chimpanzees, are not among them. Chimpanzee youngsters are hyperactive. Adult chimpanzees prefer to spend their spare time sitting down quietly grooming each other.

The behavior pattern of humans follows that of chimpanzees. At some age tennis stops being fun and turns into work. We give up mountain climbing and take up bridge. Some few humans do keep up a regular exercise pattern all of their lives, but this activity is not normal. It is reasoned activity. Most of our adults are aware that they are not getting enough exercise and resolve to take more "just as soon as I feel like it." Somehow that day never comes. As a result, our northern hospitals prepare for a rash of acute coronary cases whenever the first snowfall of the year is predicted because the unaccustomed work of snow removal will rupture heart muscles allowed to grow flabby in summertime.

There can be no doubt that humans have retained many of the instincts of our prehuman ancestors. It is also certain that humans will frequently follow their instincts even when they know better. The adult instinct to take things easy was a good instinct a few million years ago, but the changed environment has turned this once good instinct into a killer. We can console ourselves, however, by reflecting that in these cases the individuals who are lost to the population are those most enslaved to their instincts, and, hence, the ones whom the population can best do without.

The changed human environment of today has changed many other once good instincts into killers. Eventually our species will evolve to lose these bad instincts, but it will take a million years or more. It will be the elimination of those with these bad instincts that will cause the evolution of our species.

When our ancestors climbed up from the terrariums, they brought their instincts with them. In the new environment of the island, many of the older instincts could be fatal if our ancestors were not careful. Those who survived were those who were careful about following their instincts.

Every species forced into a new environment will immediately start re-evolving to meet the demands of the new environment. Some species manage the transition. Some do not, and these species become extinct. Our species arrived in an environment where it could be fatal to follow instincts. As a result, it evolved a new instinct that made it distrust following instincts.

This instinct is still active in our species. When it is triggered, we call it our conscience. This instinct is the cause

67

for the strong puritanical streak present in many of us. It is a little ironic because this new instinct itself is a true instinct, and, as such, is connected to the pleasure/pain centers in the brain. It produces a pleasurable feeling of satisfaction whenever one of the ordinary instincts is successfully resisted. However, these ordinary instincts are also operative and are also connected to the pleasure/pain centers, and the refusal to follow them produces discomfort. This ambivalence regarding our instincts is responsible for a good bit of our inner conflicts.

Our ancestors were forced into a way of life on their island, and this way of life persisted long enough to become imprinted in the genes of our species. It is not hard for us to reconstruct the way that they lived. We know they lived in rather small groups. Each group had its territory that produced the food necessary for the survival of the group. However, because all creatures breed, each territory was nearly always too small for its group. Therefore each group was continually looking for opportunities to expand its territory at the expense of one of the neighbors. (Are things different now?)

Open and overt hostilities were rare on the island if the odds were anything like even. It was far too dangerous for one group to attack another unless the odds were overwhelming. Those groups that tried it were so weakened that, even when they won, some other neighbor would find them easy prey. The normal state of affairs was a state of cold war with frequent probes to test the strengths and resolution of the neighbors.

When a species must eat certain foods to survive, sooner or later it will evolve to prefer those foods. Why? Because those individuals who like those foods the least will be relatively disadvantaged. Nature is ruthless about removing disadvantaged individuals from populations. In the same way, when a species is forced into a way of life for a long, long time to survive, that species will evolve to have preference for that way of life. Such preferences will persist even when the necessity is gone. It is not an accident that all over the world people have preferred to live in rather small groups if they have a choice. Also it is not an accident that these small groups were usually in a state of hot or cold war with all neighbors. The city-states of ancient Greece are examples, and so are the feudal systems of Europe. Empires such as Rome are not the results of the desires of average people. They are the result of the efforts of a gifted and dedicated few.

Today all primitive tribes are organized somewhat along the lines of our remote ancestors. For example, the pre-Columbian American indians had a fair approximation of such organization. But primitive tribes today all have plenty of room, while the inhabitants of our ancestral island did not.

The closest modern parallel to the way of life of our island ancestors can be found in the organization and structure of the street gangs of young males found in our cities. Each gang is organized around a male-dominated hierarchy. Each gang claims and defends a territory. Each gang is in a continual state of hot or cold war with all other gangs. The rights of others not within the gang just do not exist. All outsiders are automatically classified as enemies and/or prey.

I know that there are many sociologists who aver that these street gangs are a localized and fairly recent phenomenon, but it is not my fault that these sociologists have not studied history. If they had, they would know that every country in every age has had the equivalent of the modern American street gangs that plague Chicago and New York. The London police are bothered by their "teddy boys," who are the cultural descendants of the juvenile gangs described by Dickens in *Oliver Twist*. There are the *gamins* of Paris, the *gamines* of Bogotá, and the tsotsi of Capetown. China and Russia have their equivalents, too, calling them names that translate into "hooligans."

Why should these street gangs be universal? It is simply because with puberty, the adult instincts of every animal species become activated and take control. The instincts to form gangs are the instincts our ancestors evolved so they could survive in the environment they occupied in the past five million years. These instincts are not very desirable today, but it is futile and dangerous to think they will go away if we deny they exist. These instincts can be compared to hereditary diabetes. It cannot be cured, but it can be controlled. However, before hereditary diabetes can be controlled, it must be diagnosed.

On the island, as we have said, overt hostilities were rare. However, the group size was small. If a neighboring group could be weakened by the subtraction of a few of its fighters one at a time, it would not take long to reduce the strength of that neighbor to a point where the remainder could be safely overrun.

Every now and then this happened. Some military genius would be born into a tribe. When he grew up, he would devise strategy that would allow his tribe to overrun some neighbor. Then the combined territories would provide enough food to allow his tribe to grow. The next generation might be large enough to overrun still other neighbors, perhaps take over the entire island. Then there would be a period of peace and plenty.

However, it does not take long for any species without efficient predators to overpopulate any area, no matter how large. Sooner or later, all superbands had to break up. For a time, there might be friendship or at least tolerance between the segments of a split-up band, but memories are short, and there were ever-increasing population pressures that meant starvation, unless natural resources were defended.

Hostilities recommenced, and the same old way of life started over again with the population consisting of a number of small groups at continual odds with all others. However, each cycle made a difference. The end of each cycle found the genes of the genius that started the cycle and the genes of the tribe that bred him present within every group. Each cycle left the surviving population a little smarter. Five million years of such cycling tripled the size of the brains of our species.

We could have a lot of fun if we wished, digging into the types of strategy used by our ancestors against each other. Undoubtedly, they used all types employed by the lower animals. For example, it has been reported that young female coyotes will circle remote ranch houses at night, making love-sick noises and letting the odor of their biological condition drift over to the ranch watchdog. Male dog brains seem to turn to mush in the presence of females, so the watchdogs leave the safety of the ranch house and go out to investigate. When a dog is far enough away from the house, he is overrun by several male coyote companions of the female decoy.

On the island, a young female crying noisily on a hillside might lure an investigator from another tribe away from his friends to meet the same fate, because male human brains seem to be little better than male dog brains where females are concerned. Other types of strategy that seem simple and natural now were thought up by early geniuses, one at a time. Things like ambushes, placement of rocks that would roll down on enemies, night attacks, etc.—all followed mutations that produced slightly larger brains and more reasoning power than the average.

Here we have the reason for the rapid advance in intelligence in our species. By a geological accident our ancestors were trapped on an island where the chief threat to survival was the intelligence of others of the same species. The threats to existence that confront most species when they change environments are threats of a fairly constant magnitude. When the displaced species evolves sufficiently physically and mentally to survive, further evolution slows or stops.

Our species on the island did not face a threat of constant magnitude. Each time some group became smart enough to survive against the threat of its neighbors, that tribe used its intelligence to wipe out the threat. Soon thereafter, though, new neighbors appeared, consisting of cousins who were as smart as anybody. On the island our ancestors were engaged in a constant game of catch-up, but they could never catch up.

The way of life for five million years on the island left its marks in the genes of our species. Each group was necessarily organized into a semimilitary type of organization. Today every business and organization is arranged along similar lines. We dream of cooperative organizations where everyone knows what to do and does it without direction, but such systems are so alien to our nature that none have worked.

Some people today are quite happy living or working in a group organized along military lines. However, a mere five million years, even in an environment where evolution is rapid, is a mighty short time to completely impress a new way of life on a species. But this five million years certainly gave our species the ability to be able to tolerate a military-type lifestyle for a considerable time without creating much trauma. People are able, even willing, to put up with a lot of what they don't like in order to be able to do what they do like. Think of all the trouble, discomfort, and expense a man will happily put up with to get to kill a duck or deer.

Our modern males come by their hunting instincts honestly. For five million years, and perhaps more, our male ancestors were hunters, but the game that they hunted was often game not like ducks and deer. Our ancestors hunted the most dangerous game of all, and the danger undoubtedly contributed to the excitement and enjoyment of the pastime. Today duck and deer hunters, armed with shotguns, hide themselves before dawn in places where their prey are known to pass. Our ancestors, armed with rocks, hid themselves before dawn on cliff edges overlooking trails where strangers were known to pass.

Now we come to the cooperative effort of a number of males to wipe out some sufficiently weakened neighboring tribe that possessed natural resources the first tribe would like to have. We call this war. Wars were a necessary way of life for our male ancestors for millions of years—long enough for instincts to arise to enjoy wars as an end in themselves, especially since the required activities of wars were not far out of line with the activities of our ancestors for many millions of years before they arrived on their island home. Of course wars were not much fun for the losers. But the losers did not survive, so their opinion does not matter.

We are all descended from an incredibly long line of winners. Our instincts regarding wars are the instincts of winners. Wars, to our remote ancestors, were times when they could cast off all the restraints imposed upon them in their daily lives. Wars were times when our male ancestors could let go and do whatever their instincts prompted them to do. Wars were times when they were free to kill strange men, steal the possessions of these strange men, and rape the strange females. (Any strange female was always fair game for our remote ancestors. Now you can see why a strange female today evokes instant lust in many modern men.)

Once a species has acquired any characteristic, that characteristic will not readily leave the species, even though the environment might change to remove the necessity for that characteristic. It was necessary for our ancestors to war against all strangers, and the instincts regarding wars are still with our species. Here is a description of a fairly recent, typical war, extracted from Chapter 31 of the Book of Numbers.

"And they warred against the Midianites, as the Lord commanded Moses; and they slew all the males. . . . And the children of Israel took *all* the women of Midian captives, and their little ones, and took the spoil of all their cattle, and all their flocks, and all their goods. And they burnt all their cities wherein they dwelt, and all their goodly castles, with fire. . . . And they brought the captives, and the prey, and the spoil, unto Moses. . . . And Moses was wroth. . . . And Moses said unto them, Have ye saved all the women alive? . . . Now therefore kill every male among the little ones, and kill every woman that hath known man by lying with him. But all the women children, that have not known a man by lying with him, keep alive for yourselves."

With minor variations, the war with the Midianites could have taken place four or five million years ago. Actually, it occurred thirty-two or thirty-three centuries back. The weapons of warfare have changed since then, but the time interval between then and now is far too brief for evolution to have made any changes in the fighters. As those soldiers were then, so ours are now; at least ours would be that way if they were let.

Well, perhaps modern soldiers have some slightly thicker veneer of civilization, but don't bet your life on that veneer holding up. There are almost exact parallels between the war with the Midianites and the fighting in Asia Minor in the 1920s, and in the fighting in Africa in the last ten years. In fact, pick almost any place in the world, and almost any time period, and you can find parallels. Even the policies of the Puritans, in their wars against the Indians, were patterned after the policies of Moses. So were those of Custer and Cortez.

CHAPTER 8

FROM *HOMO HABILIS*
TO *HOMO SAPIENS*

F OR ALL THAT was mentioned in the last chapter, our species might still be living on the Mediterranean island where it evolved its intelligence. This chapter will cover the exodus.

To answer the question of how our ancestors were able to leave their island home, all we need to do is remember that ice ages have been coming and going like clockwork for at least the last two hundred million years. Records of these ice ages are contained in the layers of the microscopic seashells found in the cores extracted from the seabeds by the *Glomar Challenger* and ships like her. Each shell was produced by a tiny creature that had, and still has, a preferential water temperature. By the changes in the types of shells and by the thickness of the layers, our scientists can determine fairly accurately when each ice age occurred and how long it lasted.

In each ice age so much water is locked up in glaciers that the water level of all the oceans falls considerably. In ice ages, the continental shelves are exposed, and islands on the shelves become mountains. The dropping of the sea level causes rivers all over the world to run faster, and these rivers carve deep canyons in the continental shelves. These canyons still exist; however, they are now underwater. The Hudson canyon, for example, is a prominent feature of the underwater scenery near New York. The last ice age lowered the seas by only 240 feet, but the evidence of the underwater river can-

75

yons reveals that previous ice ages undoubtedly lowered the seas much more.

After the Mediterranean Sea reflooded, and our ancestors were trapped on an island, it was only a question of time before an ice age came along. The waters of the Mediterranean fell. An escape route opened up.

We must keep in mind that when an escape route opened up, our ancestors did not consider it an escape route. It is a law of nature that a species will not willingly change environments. So when it became possible to leave the island, who left? Was it the dominant clans that had everything their own way? Of course not! It was the second-class citizens who had no choice but to leave or die.

The first emigrants from the island found out when they came ashore that, second-class citizens or not, they were vastly superior to anything else in the world. Oh, some of the larger predators could not be faced, but these could be avoided. As far as the smaller animals were concerned, the first emigrants found that the animals were easier prey than anything they had ever hunted before. There was vegetable food in abundance. To celebrate, the first emigrants multiplied as fast as they could and spread out all over the earth. It is certain these emigrants had retained their instincts to kill strangers, but they also had acquired instincts to use considerable prudence. So, since there was plenty of room, instead of fighting, the bands moved on when a neighborhood became crowded.

World history repeated. The climate changed. A warm spell melted the glaciers and the sea level rose. The escape route from the home island to the mainland was cut off. As far as those ashore were concerned, the mechanics of evolution kept the mainlanders from evolving further, but on the island, those that were retrapped by the rising waters soon overpopulated their homeland again. A new period of rapid evolution set in for the islanders as they repeated their history over and over.

History continued to repeat. After a few score thousand

years of relatively warm weather, a new ice age arrived. The waters of the Mediterranean fell. The escape route reopened. A new group of emigrants was forced from the island to the mainland.

When the second wave of emigrants reached the mainland, it is certain they encountered the descendants of the first wave. It is doubtful these mainlanders were recognized as long lost cousins. They were recognized as strangers. Not just as strangers, either, but as strangers so relatively dumb that they could be safely killed. So as the second wave multiplied and spread out, the descendants of the first wave were eliminated wherever and whenever they were encountered.

History continued to repeat. Warm spells alternated with ice ages. In each warm spell those that were left on the island settled down to a few more eons of rapid evolution, while those out in the world stagnated. Each new ice age set loose a vastly higher evolved species of *Homo* to conquer the world.

The creatures whom we call *Homo habilis* were the descendants of one of the earlier waves of emigrants. *Homo habilis* was able to spread out as far away as Africa. There *Homo habilis* found many animal species that were rather large and fairly easy to kill. Among these animals was a bipedal creature that we now call the australopithicene. These pin-headed creatures were just another prey animal as far as *Homo habilis* was concerned, and neither *Homo habilis* or any other variety of *Homo* was ever a conservationist. Too many millions of years of near starvation had created instincts to acquire any animal food available, as quickly as possible. Of course this was a good instinct on the island and down in the terrariums because the opportunity to kill something was rather rare. In those restricted environments there was just no chance to kill more than could be used before hunger set in again.

Out in the world, though, killing was easy, and those people indulged their instincts. Keep in mind that our relatively recent westerners would kill a buffalo for just a couple pounds of the choicest meat. On the early cross-country trains, the conductors made a little extra money renting rifles to the passengers so the passengers could have some fun shooting buffalo from the moving train windows. We should not criticize *Homo habilis* for exterminating a species of giant pig, a type of giant sheep as big as cows, and those pin-headed creatures now called Australopithecus. We are more evolved, in some ways, than *Homo habilis,* but we still share the same instincts. Anyway, *Homo habilis* got his just deserts soon after the next wave of emigrants came ashore from the home island.

This account of our prehistory has now solved one of the major mysteries of anthropology. The paleontologists have assembled sets of bones of many species of animals, and it has been noted that the evolution of animals is a smooth, gradual, almost imperceptible process. However, with prehuman bones and artifacts, too, the advances in evolution seemed to have come in abrupt jumps like stair steps without transitional forms. Sometimes, too, primitive bones and artifacts have been found that overlie more evolved relics. Well, why not? It took thousands of years for each wave of emigrants to wipe out all of the descendants of an earlier wave. After *Homo habilis* was through with a territory and had moved on, a band of less evolved creatures could have moved in to occupy the hunting campsites of *Homo habilis.*

History continued to repeat. An ice age released upon the world those creatures we now call Neanderthal. All previous varieties of *Homo* vanished. Neanderthal men ruled supreme for many thousands of years. The Neanderthal were almost human. They made very good weapons and tools. However, if dating methods are to be trusted, it is interesting to note that Neanderthal artifacts, made a full sixty thousand years apart, show almost no improvement in design.

The last ice age (so far) was not really an ice age; it was more like three ice ages in rapid succession, with peaks (nadirs?) roughly 75,000, 50,000, and 25,000 years ago. Those creatures whom we call Cro-Magnon came ashore in the first or second of these peaks. Cro-Magnon weapons are a quantum jump more advanced than Neanderthal weapons. Neanderthal man promptly vanished. Those creatures whom we call European modern men came ashore, probably in the third phase of the last ice age, with the benefits of up to fifty thousand years of rapid evolution beyond that of Cro-Magnon. Cro-Magnon promptly vanished.

Homo habilis, Neanderthal, etc., were not our ancestors. Each represents a sample of the stage of evolution achieved by our ancestors at the height of an ice age. Each of these earlier types of prehumans stagnated because they found physical environments in which they could survive without much trouble, and they were able to set up fairly stable social environments. Our species, however, has not been able to set up a stable, unchanging social environment. Therefore we can expect that our species, unlike Neanderthal, et al., is still evolving. The only question is—in what direction?

CHAPTER 9

THE FORMATION OF RACES

WE WILL NOW take up the formation of the various human races. We will not attempt to define what a race is, other than to say it is a group of persons with fairly common characteristics and ancestry. We will not even try to say how many races there are, or even what constitutes a race. These definitions belong to the area of interest of ethnologists, who all have good reasons for their various definitions regarding races, even if they don't agree. Some ethnologists say there are thirty-plus races. Others say there are only three. All can prove their points.

How does a species become split into fairly distinct and separate groups? There are several methods. First let's take another look at Darwin's finches. The first finches to arrive on the Galápagos islands found a number of empty ecological niches. The original population evolved to fill all of these empty niches, forming separate varieties as they evolved. This is one method of turning a species into several species. Of course Darwin's finches never evolved far enough along their separate paths to become separate species, but they would have if given enough time. As it is, they diverged more sharply than the human races have.

Darwin's finches lived in a very special type of environment, and it is very improbable that any species that lives in a normal environment could split the way they did. For one thing, in a normal environment there just have not been any empty ecological niches for probably hundreds of millions of years.

Even though there are no empty ecological niches in a normal environment, there are some niches that are quite wide. Some individuals, by chance, are certainly somewhat better at exploiting the food sources at one end of the niches than at the other. Given enough time, a species can divide up an ecological niche into two niches and become two varieties, or species, as it does so. For example, think of the wolves and coyotes. They came from a common stock that preyed on many different-sized animals. Now the wolves and coyotes are diverging, with the wolves taking the large animal end of the ecological niche and the coyotes the small-prey animal end. This method of forming new varieties, however, takes a fantastically long time. Far too long to be the way *Homo sapiens* split into races.

Ethnologists are in fair agreement that the reason for the development of the various races of humanity is that certain segments of the human populations became physically separated from the rest and evolved, for a short distance, along some not quite parallel tracks. This has happened to some animal species. Portions of an animal species can become isolated by a river, a mountain range, or a desert. But these natural barriers have not stopped prehumans all the way back to the time of Ramapithecus, so the ethnologists have not been able to come up with the mechanism that isolated portions of our species for long enough times to create the various races. With our new way of looking at prehistory, though, we will do it for them.

To account for the various races of humanity, let's go back five and a half million years to the time when the ancestors of all of us were living on a Mediterranean island. At that time our ancestors were a fairly homogeneous group. Then an ice age arrived, and some of the islanders moved to the mainland.

Let's follow these first emigrants as they multiplied and spread out. Their first requirement was a food supply. Actually, food was not much of a problem for them almost anywhere in the outside world, but they didn't know that.

However, they did know where they could find food. Many generations of near starvation on an island had certainly made them familiar with the foods that could be obtained from the sea. They knew which seaweeds were edible. They could gather shellfish. Probably they could catch crabs, octopus, and some fish.

It is certain that when the first emigrants left their island home some of the bands followed the shorelines as they multiplied and spread out. This was a time of an ice age, remember, and the ice ages lasted thousands of years, so the shorelines that the first emigrants followed were hundreds of feet below modern shorelines.

The emigrants covered great distances as they moved, but they took thousands of years doing it. When they came to a place where there was an abundance of food, they camped there for centuries, moving on only when they had to.

As all things must, the ice age came to an end. The waters of all the seas rose at a rate of a few inches per century, possibly up to three feet per century. Still it was inevitable that some bands that had been inching their way around the outer edges of peninsulas would awake some morning and find themselves trapped on newly formed islands. At about this same time, of course, the escape route from the original home island was also closed.

Promptly, after each group found themselves trapped on an island, they overpopulated their home. The overpopulation caused the law of the survival of the fittest to resume in its most elemental form, and the fittest were the smartest. Evolution had essentially stopped for our species. So long as it was possible to spread out, even the least intelligent found it easy to survive.

Rapid evolution recommenced on all inhabited islands, and from that time on, there was not just one home island, there were many. The chief threat to the survival of any group on any island was the intelligence of neighboring groups on the island. All islanders evolved in the direction of increased intelligence.

However, since no two islands were exactly the same, subsequent evolution was not exactly parallel. Furthermore, while the rate of evolution on all inhabited islands was rapid, it was faster on some than on others. The larger the island, for example, the more it resembled a normal environment where evolution is slow, simply because of the distances a new, beneficial mutation had to travel to become common to the population and because of the large numbers in the population. On islands where diseases, hostile animals, and other inimical natural forces kept the prehuman population down, evolution was also rather slow.

Eventually the interglacial warm spell came to an end. Another ice age lowered the waters and opened escape routes. Bands of emigrants left each island for the mainland. There they encountered the descendants of those who had gone ashore and stayed ashore. These mainland creatures had not evolved appreciably during the thousands of years of the interglacial period. The emerging, more highly evolved islanders found the mainlanders easy prey. The mainlanders vanished. Eventually, the expanding groups from the various islands met. Those that met as equals survived.

The diverse groups of humans we have discussed so far were of different races. However, these original races were not the present-day races. They came later.

History continued to repeat itself. Each of the original races spread out to take over the world. You will recall that, with just a 2 percent annual increase in population, two people will turn into nearly a billion in a thousand years, so it did not take too long to fill up the world. We can be certain that our peripatetic and ubiquitous progenitors got themselves into every place they could reach as they looked for a place of their own. These places, of course, included all offshore islands that were part of the mainland during any ice age. There some groups were trapped anew by the rising waters of the next interglacial warm spell.

A casual glance at the charts of the world reveals many hundred of islands that are parts of the mainlands in the ice ages. The Mediterranean Sea is filled with such islands. (This is probably why there seems to be so many European races today.) Outside of the Mediterranean area, going east, there is Ceylon, now called Sri Lanka. Next are the Andaman Islands, which were bumps on a vast plain in the ice ages. The continental shelf of southeast Asia is loaded with mountains that are now the islands of Sumatra, Java, Bali, Borneo, etc. It just might have been possible to reach the Philippines. Turning north, the islands of Hainan and Taiwan were connected to China, and it was also possible to walk across from Korea to Japan.

All islands that could be reached in an ice age were undoubtedly reached, and these islands turned into traps at the start of the next interglacial periods. The lack of fossils need not bother us. Fossils will not form just anywhere. However, Eugène Dubois did find prehuman fossils on Java. These creatures were given the name of *Pithecanthropus erectus.* There is a lot of argument about how advanced these creatures were, but there should not be any argument about the fact that Pithecanthropus did not swim to Java. No, these creatures walked over there when the Sunda shelf was dry land. Incidentally, it is extremely unlikely that New Guinea and Australia were reachable by walking, even though there is evidence that the first of the aborigines got there about thirty thousand years ago—and that was certainly during an ice age.

On many islands, no doubt, the trapped human population became extinct before the next ice age opened an escape route. However, on every island where humans survived, they also evolved. At the end of each interglacial period, history repeated. Diverse groups of highly evolved people came ashore and found the less evolved mainlanders easy prey. The mainlanders promptly became extinct. Inevitably, the emerging races met. Those that met as equals survived.

The last ice age formed escape routes about 75,000, 50,000, and 25,000 years ago. Every mainland race today is at least 25,000 years old and may be as much as 75,000 years old. In either case, this is a very long time for the races, whatever they are, to have survived as races. So, while it would be easy to end this chapter here, the continued existence of the various races for so long a time is significant, and we will go on to explore the reasons why there is more than one human race today.

Before discussing humans, let's go into the reasons why the animal equivalents of races are able to maintain their separate integrity. Let's look at wolves and coyotes. Their habitats overlap. These creatures are close enough kin to crossbreed and enjoy it, so it might be thought that at the boundaries of their ranges one species would gradually merge into the other. However, this is just not so. Crosses between wolves and coyotes do occur, but they are rare. And it is very unlikely that you will ever see wolf/coyote crosses except in the artificial environment of a zoo. The crosses, while fertile, are not viable.

Why should crosses be rare? It is because life in the wild is hard. Nearly every predator is hungry most of the time. Wolves kill and eat all nonwolves and fairly often even eat each other. The same is essentially true of coyotes. So, while they can and do enjoy crossbreeding, the two species just do not trust each other. Chance encounters are more likely to result in dinner for one than a honeymoon for two. However, when a pair meets by accident at the psychological moment, and the two happen to be well fed, there is socialization.

When the half-bred pups arrive, these pups, like all creatures, inherit a random half of their characteristics from each parent. Instincts are inheritable characteristics, and the heads of both wolves and coyotes are packed with instincts. Furthermore, while both wolves and coyotes are considered smart animals, much of this smartness is due to their instincts. Life in the wild is harsh, and every wolf and coyote pup needs every one of its instincts to survive, and, even so, the majority do not survive for long. So, since wolf/coyote crosses have half the instincts of each parent, they cannot have the full set of instincts of either. Half-bred pups may have the physical equipment necessary for survival, but they cannot have the mental equipment to survive in the environment of either parent.

When mama stops feeding the products of her miscegenation, they starve. At least they would starve if they were let. Actually, the pups would not look right, act right, or smell right in the opinion of their full-blooded cousins, and these creatures consider everything that does not seem exactly right to them as food. Wolves that are injured so that they cannot act normally, for example, are promptly recycled through the pack. So the most likely fate of crossbred pups is to end up as a dinner for a cousin. Meat is meat.

In the foregoing illustration of how natural forces keep varieties of animals separate, we were speaking of natural environments. However, due to the activities of men, natural environments are becoming scarce. In the resulting artificial environments, natural forces have a somewhat different effect. For example, due to the advance of civilization, the environment of the red wolves and of the coyotes of Texas and Louisiana is no longer an environment that either species evolved to inhabit. Furthermore, the physical environments no longer just overlap. They coincide. This leaves the red wolves and the coyotes occupying the same ecological niche. Whenever this happens, one species is doomed. In this case it is the wolves, because, while both species are disadvantaged, the wolves are disadvantaged the most.

The larger prey animals that are preferred by the wolves are now scarce. The preferential prey of coyotes is not. Also, wolves generally must have fresh meat, while the coyotes are content with carrion. In this artificial situation, when crosses occur, the crosses, because of their coyote genes, have a better chance to survive than the pure wolves. Some do survive, and these crosses seem viable. However, this is an illusion. After the wolves are gone, the crosses will be in direct competition with the pure coyotes, and then the wolf genes will be handicaps. The crosses will vanish.

Now, at long last, we return to humans to explore the

reason why the races, whatever they are, have endured as well and for as long as they have. The reason, of course, is that the same natural forces that keep varieties of animals separate also tend to keep varieties of humans separate.

Humans may be one species. However, the various races certainly have different physical characteristics. The differences permit some types to live comfortably in physical environments where others would be handicapped.

These characteristics have nothing to do with intelligence. It is not lack of intelligence that has caused big-nosed people to be extremely scarce among the natives of the far north. Going on, the sun that feels good to a Bushman can kill a Nordic, through skin cancer if nothing else. A Nordic cannot live as a Bushman in the environment of the Bushman, regardless of how intelligent he is. There are extreme examples, true. But every individual who lives in any physical environment that is different from the environment inhabited by his (or her) ancestors for a few thousand years back is going to be at some disadvantage in competition with the natives. In the long run, the disadvantaged individuals will slip toward the lower subsistence levels of any society, animal, or human, and eventually vanish.

The social environment plays a large part in keeping the races separate, too. As each race came ashore in the last ice age, it brought with it all of the differing characteristics that had evolved as the race formed. On each island, for example, there were foods available. The islanders evolved to be able to survive on those foods, and they also evolved to enjoy those foods. These racial food preferences persist today. True, the native foods of one race are frequently relished by other races, but it is also true that foods containing everything necessary for the existence of one race may be inadequate for members of another. Not only that, many foods routinely eaten by one race may be actually poisonous to others.

Let's digress briefly to discuss one of the dietary peculiarities of our species. As you probably know, people of European descent use a lot of dairy products. However, this is not true of the world's population as a whole. There are vast areas where 80 to 100 percent of the native adult population have no use for milk as a food. (This was not discovered until shortly after World War II, when it was noticed that tons of powdered milk sent to relieve food shortages were left to rot on the docks.)

As children, the natives of those places can drink milk. But with maturity, the body chemistry changes, and they no longer can tolerate lactose. If one of those people were to drink a glass of milk, he or she would get violently sick—at both ends. Such a person would certainly be handicapped if he or she tried to live in Europe on the diet of Europeans. Now you can see why minority groups in many societies cling to their native foods. It is not just that they prefer them. They need them.

Let's digress further to discuss the reason why so many adult humans cannot drink milk. Whenever we encounter any characteristic such as this one—common to a large portion of the population, we can be sure that it is not an accident. There is a reason, and this reason is that somehow, in some environment, that characteristic was an aid to survival. The inability to make use of any food source would seem to be a disadvantage, though, in this environment, so let's look at the environment just preceding.

On the islands where the races were formed, we may be certain that there were near-continual overpopulation problems. A famine would reduce the population for a time. Then the next generation or so would build up the population to where there would be another famine. In times of famine, the children are traditionally the first to die. The adults take all of the food. However, here and there on some islands, there were adults that could not use milk as food. Their children had a better than average chance to survive, and any advantage, no matter how small, will eventually become common to a population. When the descendants of those lucky children came ashore to be races, they all brought the mementos of those terrible times with them in their genes.

Here is something to think about. Although the inability to tolerate lactose is rare among those of European descent, there is a small percentage with this condition. We must presume that there were some with this condition on the islands that produced the European races. We can be certain, too, that on these islands there were overpopulation problems. So why didn't this condition spread and become common? We must conclude that on the islands that produced the European races, the inhabitants found some other race survival mechanism. The reader is free to speculate on what this characteristic might be.

Each race, subrace, ethnic group, culture, subculture, etc., has created artificial environments consisting of numerous artificial ecological niches. Each of these artificial units was created to fit the needs and capabilities of the creators. Outsiders with different preferences and capabilities are frequently handicapped in competition with the natives in any ecological niche. Once again, these handicaps do not necessarily have anything to do with intelligence. To begin with, each race, subrace, etc., created a language for itself out of sounds that were easy for the creators to produce. However, the different types of humans have different types of throats, tongues, lips, etc., and the sounds that are easy for one may be impossible for another. The Chinese have trouble with the English *r* sound. The English have trouble with the Bantu click. Trouble with the spoken language is a severe handicap for minorities. Going on, the musical sounds enjoyed by one race, culture, etc., may be just meaningless sounds to another. The dances, amusements, art forms, etc., of one may be incomprehensible to another. The inherited resistance to diseases varies considerably between ethnic groups. All these things keep groups from merging and also handicap some individuals in their competition with the natives.

A large number of people have predicted that in the far future the human population will be a homogeneous mixture of all the races that exist today. The prediction can never come

89

true. It is a biological impossibility. To begin with, racial characteristics are inherited. Like all inherited characteristics, racial characteristics are encoded within our genes. The amount of data that the genes of any one person can contain is limited. If the future population is approximately homogeneous, their genes will be approximately homogeneous also, and therefore a large number of the present genes and racial characteristics will necessarily have vanished from the population.

Which of the present genes would have vanished? It would be the ones that produced relative handicaps, of course. But the survivability of an individual does not depend upon just one or two characteristics. It is the entire gestalten of all. (The whole is greater than the sum of its parts.) Two varieties of any species in any environment cannot be equal in their ability to survive within that environment. Mixing the two varieties does not create a third variety. It only creates a mixture with a chance combination of characteristics from both. True, some of these mixtures may contain combinations of characteristics that produce superior individuals, but these superior individuals cannot start a new variety, because the laws of genetics keep these mixtures from breeding true. Of course, while nature could not produce a superior race, it is possible that humans can. We may be able to clone some superior individuals and use them to start a new race.

Predicting the future is not one of the objectives of this book. But describing evolution is, and one of the aspects of evolution is the shifts in the composition of a population following the introduction of two varieties (or more) into a single environment. If we look at what has happened in the past, whenever this happened, we can determine the most probable future, assuming nature has her way, for our species. Of course, evolution is normally far too slow to observe, but you will recall that there are environments where evolution is rapid. These are rather small and isolated places, but the world has many islands that meet this criteria.

For example, the Dutch discovered the island of Tasmania

in 1642. Soon after, the population of Tasmania consisted of Europeans, plus the native islanders. Today that native population is extinct. The present population of Tasmania may contain a few of the genes of the natives, but they seem to be vanishing. For another example, Columbus discovered the Caribbean Islands in 1492. They were inhabited by the Carib Indians. Soon the Caribs were extinct. At about the time the Caribs vanished, the Europeans imported African natives. Today the Caucasian population on many of the Caribbean islands is virtually extinct. The mulatto population seems to be shrinking. Pick some islands for yourself and check the trends in the composition of the population. The trends seem unmistakable. These same trends are taking place worldwide, too, even though in most of the world the trend is too slow to observe.

The human species is a species that has been displaced from the environment that it evolved to inhabit. This has happened to many species in the past. All followed the same pattern. The original displaced population, either plant or animal, was fairly homogeneous, but not adapted to the new environment. Chance mutations that produced advantages started the species evolving in different directions. Some varieties found ecological niches of their own and evolved further to become new species. Those varieties that competed within a single ecological niche, though, became less numerous, and eventually only one variety was left per ecological niche. Our species is following this same pattern. Unless our species learns to avoid natural laws, our species will continue to follow the pattern.

We have not mentioned racial prejudice as a force that keeps the races apart. Racial prejudice certainly has an effect, humans being what we are. But even if prejudice could be made to vanish, the other forces of nature will inexorably preserve those best fitted for survival within any ecological niche or environment and, at the same time, these natural forces will eliminate all others.

CHAPTER 10

HAIR AND TEETH

L ET'S GO DOWN into the terrariums again and take a closer look at those early settlers who were our ancestors. There we will follow our ancestors as they evolved to exchange their apelike characteristics for ours.

But first, who were these creatures? We are not going to answer this question directly. Of course you already know that I think that they were a band of Proconsul. But there is no point in being too positive about the modern nomenclature of the species of the first involuntary settlers in the terrariums.

It is sufficient to note that scientists have taken hard looks at the structures of modern humans and have noted that there are many traces of an earlier design of a creature that lived in trees. The scientists have taken these traces and redesigned our structures on paper, shifting a connection here and relocating a joint there to make our structures more efficient from an engineering standpoint. This work is something like evolution in reverse. The result is a creature so much like Proconsul that, if it is not actually Proconsul, the differences make no difference. At least not for the purposes of this book. Further, Proconsul was so similar to modern chimpanzees that, when we want to describe some features of Proconsul, we can describe chimpanzee features, and it will be close enough.

At this point I must digress because far too many people think that chimpanzees are just cute little affectionate creatures. Well, they are, but only while they are young. The chimpanzee actors you see on stage and in jungle movies are all juveniles. Adult chimpanzees cannot be trained to be actors. They are smart enough, sure, but when they mature, their adult instincts become activated, and they will not mind anymore. Their adult instincts make them actively resist any attempts at control, too.

Adult chimpanzees stand about five feet tall and are immensely stronger than humans. They can pull an arm off an adult human. They have done it. Their fangs can puncture a human skull. They have done it. It is not just dangerous to keep a sweet little chimpanzee pet after it matures, it is fatal.

One of the most obvious differences between humans and chimpanzees (Proconsul) is their teeth. It was the environment of the terrariums that caused the change. We carry the end result of the change in our mouths.

It is hardly necessary to describe modern human teeth; all of us probably know enough of what our teeth are like. It is sufficient to know that human upper teeth are almost identical with the corresponding lowers. There are no pronounced gaps between our teeth, and the tops of all teeth are at about the same level. At least this is how our teeth are supposed to be, even though our orthodontists are getting rich correcting nature's mistakes. Our teeth, more than any other feature, seem prone to mutations. This is probably because the design of our teeth is so new that this design is not yet firmly engraved within our genes to the exclusion of all other designs.

Twenty million years back our ancestors' teeth were like the teeth of chimpanzees. Like humans, the chimpanzees have four incisor teeth in the front of each jaw. There the resemblance ends.

In the chimpanzee's upper jaw, there is a big gap between the incisors and the canine teeth. The long lower canine teeth fit up into these gaps whenever a chimpanzee closes its mouth. The chimpanzee upper canine teeth are far too long to fit into a gap in the lower jaw teeth. Instead, the upper fangs are offset so that they go outside the lower first premolars when a chimpanzee shuts its mouth. This isn't all. Each time a chimpanzee opens or shuts its mouth, the upper fangs rub on the edges of the premolars, and this rubbing creates and maintains a razor-sharp edge on the fangs. The premolars have been modified to make them efficient whet rocks.

If you look at the skull of a chimpanzee, you can see that the upper fangs are lined up with the head bones, so that if the lower jaw is swung down out of the way, the upper fangs can be used as pickaxes. This is what chimpanzees do when they fight, too. They do not bite their opponents as you or I might. Instead they open their mouths wide and swing their exposed fangs at their foes, getting the full weight of the skull and the full strength of the neck muscles into the blow.

The fangs can penetrate bones. If the fangs are buried in meat, a twist of the head causes the fangs to slice like twin butcher knives. Incidentally, now we can see why chimpanzees have flat noses. A protruding nose would be smashed flat by their instinctive method of fighting. Human noses did not evolve, could not have evolved, until after our species lost its fangs.

Today chimpanzees are considered to be rather peaceful and nonaggressive toward each other. Well, they may be now, but the frightful weaponry within their mouths is proof that this was not always so.

Features such as fangs do not evolve by accident. They evolve by use. Or rather, by long residence in an environment where their frequent use is an aid to survival. However, all chimpanzees today are about equally armed, and in a real fight, even the winner would be severely injured.

The chimpanzees have evolved to have considerable prudence in their dealings with each other. In a way, the society of the chimpanzee can be compared with some hypothetical human society where everyone is armed and ready to fight if sufficiently provoked.

People tend to be quite polite to each other in approximations of such a society. Think back to the times when an insult resulted in pistols for two at dawn, followed by breakfast for one. But getting back to chimpanzees, humans and other predators have reduced their numbers to a point where they do not overpopulate their environment. Furthermore, their females are promiscuous. With no particular food or female problems, what do they have to fight about?

Chimpanzees are essentially vegetarians. When they hunt and kill animals to eat, they use their hands for the killing. So why did the fangs evolve in the first place? The fangs are obviously fighting weapons, but whom did the ancestors of the chimpanzees have to fight with? It was not the larger predators, such as the saber-toothed, because, frightful as a chimpanzee's fangs are, they are no match for the larger meat-eaters.

Features must be successful modifications to evolve. Besides, the ancestors of chimpanzees were fairly safe from all animals after they learned to live in trees. Safe from all species, that is, but one: their own.

The fangs of Proconsul's ancestors evolved for use against others of the same species. Of course this was back in the days when they were reasonably safe from predators, so they multiplied and overpopulated their environment. Competition for survival was competition against each other. Survival meant getting more than your share of an inadequate food supply, and the fangs were a big help in this competition.

When you get right down to basics, the greatest threat to the existence of any individual animal has often been the presence of others of the same species. Every animal species can survive against the forces of nature and normal predators—human predators excepted. These species would not have survived to become species otherwise. But every species has the capability to overpopulate its environment, and they do.

Then there is a food shortage. The food that one individual gets is denied to another, who may thereby become so weakened that he or she falls easy prey to disease or predators.

In response to this threat to existence, many species of

animals have evolved to have weapons that are not of much value, except for use on others of the same species. There are some exceptions, but, generally speaking, any weapons possessed by any species, not used in food gathering, evolved to be used on others of the same species.

The spurs on the heels of chickens evolved to kill chickens. The tusks of elephants evolved to fight elephants. The horns of rhinoceroses are used against all creatures, true, but rhinoceroses also have fangs that seldom, if ever, are used except for close-up fighting with each other.

Deer grow antlers that are useless as weapons until it is time for them to be used on other deer at the mating season. Incidentally, be careful of deer at those times. The males go crazy and charge at anything that moves. (Even deer hand-raised as pets can be dangerous.) Some deer, like the musk deer of Asia, do not have antlers, but the males have fangs, which they seem to enjoy using on each other.

Goat horns evolved to settle arguments between goats. Antelope horns evolved to be used against antelope. Oh, a lucky impala might impale a lion, but this happens so infrequently that it cannot be considered the reason horns evolved. Features must be generally successful to evolve, and impala horns are generally successful only in disputes between impala.

At one time it was thought the horned animals of the great African herds had something "noble" about their characters, because, while a lot of fights were observed, there were few fatalities. But then it was learned that the large herds are really collections of small herds, and there is not much interplay between these small groups.

The animals that were observed fighting were usually close kin. They had known each other and had been fighting with each other from infancy. Under such circumstances one or the other was allowed to give up. But animal collectors soon learned not to corral together animals of the same species who were strangers to each other. Under such circumstances the males would fight, and the result was murder.

Whenever a species uses its offensive weapons on others of the same species, we frequently find that the species has evolved defensive features for protection against those offensive weapons. For example, the manes of lions are obviously a good defense against teeth, but what animal is going to be biting a lion on the neck, except another lion? The manes of horses evolved as protection against the teeth of other horses. The same reasoning applies to all excessively thick or long hairs about the necks of other species, such as the ruff found about the necks of some baboons and around the necks of wolves. You can easily extend these lists.

With the preliminaries out of the way, let's go back down into the terrariums to observe our animal ancestors. They followed the herds of grass-eaters as scavengers. Because they were just animals, they knew no better than to overpopulate their environment. It was inevitable that bands would meet at a carcass fairly often. The individuals had evolved to have considerable prudence in their dealings with each other. But hungry individuals cast prudence to the winds. When two bands met, the individuals fought. They fought as chimpanzees fight. They grappled. They opened their mouths wide and swung their protruding fangs at the throats of their opponents. The fangs cut each other's faces and necks to shreds.

In these encounters, the ones with the most facial hair suffered the least. Beards evolved as protection against the fangs. Beards were probably the first of our uniquely human features to evolve. Note that beards do not appear until maturity, when a male is old enough to be a fighter. Beards would be useless on an immature male, and useless features do not evolve.

Ever since our species lost its fangs, the beards of humans have been useless. However, remember Dollo's law. A feature will not disappear from a species just because it subsequently becomes useless. A feature must become worse than useless before a new evolutionary step will remove it. In a way, our bodies can be said to resemble some old houses where nothing is ever thrown away unless it is too dangerous to keep.

97

The first of the terrarium dwellers to have beards had an advantage. Human hair is tough, and beard hairs are the toughest of all human hair. Perhaps the beards were not a complete defense against the fangs of our species. But the beards were enough of an advantage to become common to the species. Those with beards were able to exterminate those without. (Some races today have rather skimpy beards, true, but this loss in some segments of the population came about much later because of strictly localized conditions, such as changes in the shapes of human noses, which have taken place in fairly recent years.)

We cannot say that the evolution of beards was an unmixed blessing. This new feature made it more difficult for our ancestors to kill each other. As a result, the population rose. Overall, after a few generations, there was less than ever to eat and more people to eat it.

Because following instincts could easily be fatal, the ones who managed to survive were those who were able to reason instead of having to rely completely on instincts. Then, with some reasoning ability, our ancestors learned to hunt. Not to hunt grass-eaters; they learned to hunt each other. New instincts arose to help them in this hunting, too. It is impossible for me to say how much of this hunting ability was instinctive and how much reasoned.

Well, we can't tell about leopards, either. Certainly they have hunting instincts. But they are able to modify their behavior from hunt to hunt, depending on the local circumstances. These modifications to behavior are a form of reasoning, and our ancestors have long been smarter than leopards.

We can easily arrive at the details of the earliest hunting in the terrariums. Our ancestors lived in bands normally, but the bands could not hunt as units. Hunting was a job for lone males. That meant that a hunter had to get within reach of his prey without being observed, much as a leopard will try to slip up close to a band of baboons. Next there is the selection of a victim. Even leopards do not select the adult males of a baboon tribe for victims. An infant would be fine, but infants are kept close by their mothers. The very best choice is one of the immature youngsters. Something large enough to be worthwhile, but not too large to carry off easily.

Last, there is the mode of attack. Leopards do not have much problem here. But even leopards prefer to attack from the rear so that they may be able to make their kill before the adult male guardians of the baboon band are alerted.

The hunters in the terrariums had a few more problems than leopards have with baboons. Leopards are physically capable of easily disposing of young baboons. Proconsul's fangs were terrible weapons, true. But human bodies are tough, and there are few places where the fangs could let the life out quickly and silently. In fact, from the rear, there is just one spot. This is the junction of the skull and spinal cord. A smash of the fangs into or just under the medulla oblongata would bring instant death. After the kill, there was the problem of the getaway. Perhaps the hunter was able to wiggle away, dragging his victim behind him. Perhaps he left it behind to be recovered later, because even carnivores who have no inhibitions about eating members of their own species from other bands are inhibited about eating members of their own band, unless they are very hungry of course.

Eventually nature came to the rescue of the children in the terrariums. A chance mutation produced long head hair that grew down over the vulnerable spot on the back of the neck. Long, tangled, dirty hair; hair that might not be a complete defense against the fangs but that was certainly better than the short hair on chimpanzees.

Long hair on both sexes was such an advantage in survival that it quickly became common to our species. At that time the hunting became unprofitable. There was just too much risk that the intended victim would live long enough to cry out for help. In that event, the hunters became the hunted and did not often survive. Again, it usually became fatal to follow instincts. Most of those who could not do otherwise became extinct, but not all of them.

Today, as every parent instinctively knows, there are men out in the world who are motivated to kill children and young females for no logical reason. Nearly every edition of the newspapers adds confirmation that these parents are right, too.

All I can say is what I have been saying all along. Once an instinct, or any other feature, evolves in a species, that instinct or feature will not easily leave that species. Instincts behave like long-delay time bombs passed down through the generations, just waiting for the right trigger to be touched. In this case, it is the opportunity that may be the trigger.*

After our entire species had beards and long head hair, the fangs became essentially useless as features with survival advantages. But this is not why they vanished. Remembering Dollo's law, a feature must have negative survival advantage before a new evolutionary step will make it go away. However, the required negative survival advantage was already inherent in the fangs from the first. Most evolutionary changes are compromises of a sort but they include more good than bad. In the terrariums, the good part departed, but the original remained.

What was bad about the fangs from the beginning? To answer, let's go back to the description of a chimpanzee's fangs. The lower fangs fit up into a gap between the upper teeth. The upper fangs fit close outside the lower teeth. The interlocking of the fangs and teeth means that when a chimpanzee has its mouth closed, it cannot move its jaw sideways. In short, chimpanzees cannot chew except by a straight open-and-shut motion of the mouth.

This is a very inefficient way to chew. We have a much

---

*Freud wrote, "The unconscious wish to beat or harm children is almost universal." Now you know why.

better system. We chew by a combined rotary grinding and crushing movement. This enables us, if we take time to do it, to grind up our foods very finely. Any digestive system can extract more energy out of a given amount of food that is pulverized rather than gulped down in chunks.

That isn't all. Some natural foods must be chewed thoroughly before our digestive systems can make much use of them. Some raw starches, for example. If you gulp them down, they will probably give you a bellyache. But if they are chewed thoroughly, the enzymes in saliva change the starches to sugars, and our digestive systems handle sugars very well.

Then, too, there are many tiny seeds chock-full of food energy, but the hulls of these seeds have evolved to permit the seeds to pass completely unharmed through an animal's digestive system unless the hulls are cracked. A chimpanzee might be able to survive on such seeds. But it would have to crack each hull almost individually, and it would take all day to eat enough to survive.

With our chewing system, though, we can grind up seeds by the handful. There are many more types of seeds available than most persons realize. Autopsies on thousand-year-old corpses found in the bogs of Denmark have revealed that those people ate upwards of sixty varieties of what we would call weed seeds.

It is the features of an environment that shape a species. It is changes in the environment that reshape that species. The foods available to a species are part of the environment. Form follows function in every design, including biological designs—and these include the design of teeth.

Chimpanzee teeth have not changed much in the last twenty million years. Therefore the diet of modern chimpanzees is approximately the same as the diet of Proconsul. From many observations, we know what this diet is. Chimpanzees eat fruits, flowers, buds, and berries. They also occasionally eat meat. This meat is derived from anything fairly small and available, ranging from monkeys to bushpigs to chimpanzee and baboon youngsters. All of these diverse foods have one thing in common: They do not require much chewing.

The design of human teeth is a design for efficient chewing. Such a design did not evolve by accident. Twenty million years ago, our ancestor's teeth were just about the same as modern chimpanzee teeth. So the changed design is the result of a long, long time when it was more important, from a survival standpoint, for our ancestors to chew up whatever they had to eat than to have fangs for fighting. Activities required for survival eventually evolve to become enjoyable in themselves and tend to persist long after the need is gone. Today all races of humans enjoy chewing gum, not for the flavor, but because the mechanical motion of the jaws "feels good."

With our new knowledge of the terrariums, we can go on now and dig out some more details. In the terrariums, at first, the fangs were an asset. It was not so much that they were useful in cutting up meat, though; it was because the fangs were weapons that could be used to protect any meat those scavengers found.

Then after our ancestors learned to hunt each other, the fangs were certainly an aid to survival. (The survival of the hunters, that is.) Later on, though, after our species evolved beards and long head hair, it temporarily lost its ability to function as an efficient predator of itself. Without predators, the population rose. With more people, there was a food shortage that lasted for millions of years. To stay alive, the inhabitants of the terrariums had to shift over to foods that they would not ordinarily eat. Foods that required chewing.

What foods were these? Well, let's look at the diet of starving people today. Shipwrecked sailors have prolonged their lives by eating their belts and boots. Hungry Eskimos have eaten their clothing—not the furs, of course, but the hides. In the terrariums, after the meat of an animal was gone, the once-discarded hides were chewed thoroughly to extract every particle of nourishment. Millions of years of chewing on scraps of raw hide favored the survival of those who could chew best. Chance mutations that changed the design of the teeth were aids to survival that became common to our species.

How long ago did our species lose its fangs? To answer this question we should note that the fangs of Ramapithecus were almost non-existent. From the available fossil data, we can guess that it may have been as many as eighteen million years ago when these creatures escaped from the terrariums to reenter the world and stop evolving.

It was not just chewing on hides that changed our teeth. There were some rather large animals in the terrariums and it is to be expected that sometimes a band had more meat than it could eat in several days. It was very hot and very dry in the terrariums. Any meat not promptly consumed dried out to become hard as wood.

Today you can buy strips of dried meat called jerky, and they are very tasty, indicating a very long association of our species with dried meat. You can make a meal of jerky, but it is so hard to chew that it is heavy work. Modern people who use jerky generally pound it to a powder first with a gun butt or a rock. It is probable that the first use of a rock, as a tool, was for this very purpose.

Along these lines, consider that if you use a rock to do a lot of not-very-hard pounding, you first find a rock that fits comfortably in your hand. Then, with use, the corners and bumps on that rock tend to get chipped off, leaving the rock almost perfectly round.

Almost perfectly round, baseball-sized rocks have been found in a number of prehuman camp sites. These rocks puzzle anthropologists who think that they "must have been" weapons of some sort. I wonder if the anthropologists of the far future will be equally perplexed by the meat mallets modern housewives use to make Swiss steak?

After our species lost its fangs, and not before, our ancestors were able to utilize the many plant foods that require considerable chewing to be digestible. These, too, are often made more palatable by preliminary pounding or rubbing with a rock, although quite a number can be eaten directly. For example, refer to Luke, 6:1 ". . . he went through the cornfields; and his disciples plucked the ears of corn, and did eat, rubbing *them* in *their* hands." Corn, in the sense used here, was undoubtedly available in the terrariums, but this method of making a meal would have been impossible while our ancestors still had fangs.

CHAPTER 11

THE SECOND
OLDEST PROFESSION

ONE THING LEADS to another. As each new bit is added to the jigsaw puzzle of our past, it shows the way to add more bits. The last chapter outlined the way in which our species lost its fangs and was thereby able to utilize new foods. But new foods were not all that our species gained. Modern experimenters have found, for example, that a person can gather, with bare hands, enough wild wheat grains in a couple of hours to provide food for all day or longer. So when our ancestors became able to eat grass seeds, they also acquired spare time.

Theorists have assumed that when our species acquired leisure time, the people used this leisure time to invent new things. I rather doubt this. If they did, they behaved differently from both their ancestors and their descendants. Their ancestors were Proconsul or some very similar apelike creature. Apes are not noted for using their spare time to create inventions. In fact, the adult apes are so firmly controlled by their instincts that they cannot do anything new.

At the other end of the time gap, we, their descendants, plan our leisure time very carefully so that we can use it doing things requiring a minimum of thinking. There may be some few exceptions today, but they are certainly not typical. No, we should not assume that when some adult ancestor had a full belly, he consciously devoted the time until the next meal thinking up plans for fire or the wheel. We have to look farther to find the earliest inventors.

In every society there is more than one social environment. The adults have theirs, while the children have another. The loss of the fangs and the acquisition of leisure time brought on changes in these social environments. Adults are rather set in their ways, so the changes in the adult environment were minimal. The adults spent their increased leisure time taking naps or going over to see what the girls were doing. In short, they engaged in adult activities.

In the meantime, the children spent their increased spare time in childish activities. Play. But while the preferential adult activities did not change much, the character of the play engaged in by the children underwent a drastic change.

To illustrate, let's imagine some primitive human society where every boy is given a pair of bowie knives at some early age, and the boys must have these knives with them at all times. Will these imaginary boys grow up to be proficient at knife fighting? The answer is no, because these knives are the real thing and are too dangerous to practice with. For the same reason, these boys will not grow up to be proficient in any kind of fighting, because all types of combat training have some risk of injury that might bring the knives into play.

Chimpanzee youngsters are something like these imaginary boys. They engage in games like tag and follow-the-leader, but they dare not engage in rough contact sports with their peers. This inhibition had survival value in our species, too, but only up to the time when fangs vanished. Shortly thereafter, since the young of all species are not as firmly controlled by their instincts as the adults, the children in the terrariums could, and did, play as roughly as they liked with one another. Sure, they occasionally lost their tempers and bit each other, but these bites did not produce severe injuries. In fact, without fangs it was almost impossible for the children to hurt each other very much.

However, children are persistent and inventive, and some of them managed it. Those who were hurt had an incentive to remember what it was that hurt them. (All animals learn by getting hurt; bobcats learn to leave porcupines alone, and human children learn not to poke their fingers into heaters.) In the scuffling in the terrariums, the rudiments of karate were invented, and this was the first invention.

It was probably the children who made the first physical inventions, too. Clubs were probably invented by a boy who was gnawing on a bone when he was playfully tagged by a friend. He tagged back with the bone still in his hand. Then the actual inventor of the club promptly forgot all about his invention. But the one who was tagged with the bone had a bruise to remind him of the incident for a time long enough for him to figure out the cause-and-effect relationship. So he got himself a long bone and generously shared his new found knowledge with his playmates in a way that caused them to remember what they learned. Later when they grew up, they conquered their world.

Let's go down into the terrariums for a scenario, a true scenario that recurred time after time. One morning a fangless family group is wandering over the grasslands, looking for whatever it might find. A young boy darts away in pursuit of a rabbit. Suddenly he yells. A stranger with fangs has come from behind a sand dune and has grabbed him.

The father and uncles rush to the rescue. The stranger drops the boy and tries to flee, but he has delayed too long. One of the good guys catches the bad guy by the long hair. Another of the good guys finishes the stranger off. Later, as the family is picking the bones of the stranger, possibly they discuss staking the lad out as bait to catch more would-be predators, though probably not. People at that time were not that sophisticated.

In the foregoing scenario, it was mentioned that one of the good guys held the stranger by the hair. Another of the good guys finished the stranger off. But how? Human bodies are tough, and it is very hard to kill a human quickly. But still males *are* vulnerable. The uncle disposed of the stranger by grabbing his genitals and ripping them off. The uncle had learned this technique as a boy in the youthful scuffling that came into existence only after the loss of fangs made scuffling possible. This technique had been used on the uncle himself forcibly enough for even that dim-witted creature to remember all his life. This technique could not have been learned by boys with fangs who are inhibited from contact sports. This technique helped the ones without fangs to exterminate those with fangs.

Incidentally, Eskimo boys are still taught the very same technique to use if they are surprised by a polar bear when no weapons are at hand. "Do not run," they are told, "the bear can outrun you. Instead, face the bear. It will rear up, grab you with its arms, and try to bite your head off. Raise an arm to jam into the bear's mouth to save your head. With your other hand, make a snatch at the bear's genitals and rip them off. This will discourage the bear." Eskimo hunters have saved their lives this way. Of course, if the bear is a female, the joke is on the hunter.

This same scenario also brings up another important point. The long hair on the boy saved the boy's life since it kept the stranger's fangs from puncturing his spinal cord. The long hair on the adult stranger cost the stranger his life since it provided the pursuer with a grip. So we see that long hair was a feature that evolved to have positive survival value to the young, but had negative survival value to adult males.

The stage was set, so to speak, for another evolutionary step to remove the handicap. This step actually got under way. Traces of the step exist today. Quite a number of modern males begin losing their hair at maturity. This is a hereditary condition, which we call premature baldness. It dates back to those days in the terrariums when long hair on adult males became a severe handicap in their frequent hand-to-hand fighting.

Long hair is still a handicap to a male in hand-to-hand fighting. This is not news; it has been known since history began. The boys of Sparta cut off their hair at age eight and went short haired the rest of their lives. Alexander's soldiers had closely cropped heads and beards. So did Roman soldiers.

One might wonder why a mutation with so much survival value, premature baldness, never spread to become common to our species. The answer is simple. When the mutation appeared, our ancestors were at the dawn of intelligence. They realized that a bald head on a male gave an advantage in a fight, but a naturally bald head had no advantage over an artificially bald head. The mutation that would have spread to become common to our species was nipped in the bud when men learned to give themselves haircuts.

The first haircut is too important a milestone in our prehistory to pass over lightly. Of course we cannot reconstruct each and every detail of that event, but we can present a scenario that should not be too far away from the exact truth.

The scenario opens in the terrariums about the time our species was losing its fangs. The loss of the fangs permitted out ancestors to make use of some new food sources, so for a while they had leisure time.

Did they employ their leisure in thinking up new things? Of course not. Like their ape ancestors, and like many modern humans, they employed their leisure doing the things they wanted to do—the things that made them feel good to do, the things their instincts prompted them to do. Like their ape ancestors, much of their leisure time was spent in grooming themselves and each other.

As our scene opens, a young adult male is lying on his face, and a young female is grooming him. She rubs his body with dust. The dust mixes with his and her sweat and turns into mud. She scrapes the mud off with the thin side of an old bone, possibly a rib bone, and this leaves his hide shining and clean. The male enjoys these attentions. He lies still with his eyes shut and a foolish grin on his face. The girl finishes with his body and turns her grooming to his hair.

The hair is a mess. It is long, dirty, and tangled. She cannot straighten out the tangles with her fingers, and when she tries to use the rib as a one-tooth comb, it is too large. The girl paws around in a nearby bone pile to find a more suitable tool and comes up with half an old upper jaw bone. The long fang, she thinks, will be just the thing to pick out the snarls.

When she starts using the fang, she is amazed to see that the knife edge is shearing through the hair. Fascinated with her new discovery, she gives her man a crew cut. She then rolls him over onto his back so she can get at the beard, and only then does he find out what is happening.

Was he happy about his crew cut? No, men are not like that. He was angry and beat the girl up. Soon afterward this young man was espied by some boys. These boys, like boys everywhere and everywhen, acted naturally. They jeered at the young man, calling him "Baldy."

Our hero beat them up, too, and then dragged them by the hair over to the girl and made her cut their hair. Then our hero stalked off to hide and sulk.

A little later, these new-shorn boys met some friends. These friends promptly made some remarks. In the resultant melee, the advantages of short hair became painfully apparent. So as soon as they could, all of the boys willingly lined up before the girl to get their hair cut.

The boys later kept their hair short because it felt so wonderfully cool, as well as being an advantage in a fight. It was in this way that the second oldest profession was born—the lady barber. I would like to call our heroine Delilah. But it would be inaccurate, and we must be accurate with our prehistory at all costs. Delilah did not give Samson his memorable haircut. She put him to sleep and then called a man to cut Samson's hair. (Judges 16:19)

CHAPTER 12

THE ATAVISTIC SUBCONSCIOUS

EVERY HUMAN is said to have two minds. They are the conscious mind and the subconscious mind. The literature on these mental processes indicates there is considerable mystery about them. And, in fact, there is. But if these minds are considered to be just features that evolved for specific purposes, like fingernails, eyes, and beards, much of the mystery vanishes. So without getting mired by detail, let's review the evolution of our two minds.

Long, long ago our ancestors were tiny specks of living protoplasm floating in the primordial seas. There is no point in concerning ourselves with our ancestors that far back. A few million years later, however, our ancestors had evolved into fish. On their way to becoming fish, these ancestors acquired beating hearts, eyes, digestive systems, and a good number of other appurtenances still retained by our species in one form or another. These added features were not independent packages. Each required integration and control. Nervous systems evolved to provide the integration. Brains evolved to provide the control. These brains, like modern computers, may seem to be complicated, and in a way they are; however, both brains and computers are mostly large assemblies of fairly simple circuits.

Messages come into a computer or a brain circuit, and in response, one or more messages are sent out to different places. For example, when a fish sees a bigger fish with big teeth, this sight is an optical signal that goes to a brain circuit, which immediately sends a message to the tail muscles telling them to wiggle faster. This same brain circuit also sends additional messages to other places, and these additional messages tell various body parts to provide support for the tail muscles. For instance, messages to glands release stimulants into the fish's blood.

Most of the activity of our fish ancestors was of the stimulus/response type that did not require any conscious control. Humans today still have similar stimulus/response activity. If we touch something sharp or hot by accident, our hand is jerked back without any conscious volition. This is a very good ability to have. For one thing, reflexes work faster than consciously controlled movements.

Did our fish ancestors have a consciousness? The answer must be yes. Not much, of course, but they did have senses that let them know what was going on around them. They had reflexes to take care of actions—but what actions?

These ancestors had decisions to make as to whether to dodge left or right. Should they run, or should they fight? No brain can possibly be big enough to contain inherited reflexes that are perfect solutions to all the problems of existence. So the reflexes should be considered as general solutions to the problems of survival. The consciousness comes from additional brain tissue, and its duty is to modify the reflex actions somewhat as circumstances change.

A few eons after our ancestors became fish, they crawled out of the water and became reptiles. Their bodies evolved to meet the problems of living on dry land. But did their brains change also? The answer is, certainly. But these reptile ancestors did not have to start all over again with their brains. Many of the brain circuits of the fish were still perfectly useful—circuits that controlled things like swallowing and elimination, for example. So while new brain circuits evolved in the reptiles, the greater part of the fish brain was retained. It is still retained.

Our ancestors went through many additional evolutionary steps, but each change of their bodies kept all of the previous brain circuits that were still useful. In fact, each step keeps all the brain circuits that become merely useless. Remember Dollo's law, which states that features that once evolve in a species will not be lost to the species, unless a changed environment makes those features handicaps!

So today we have in the backs of our heads the remnants of a fish brain. Over and in front of this brain is a reptile brain. Then there is an early mammal brain, a few other brains, and also the greater part of the brain of an anthropoid ape. Each of these brains is a collection of circuits of nerve cells, and these circuits are still performing the same functions they always did.

If you would like an example of a useless control circuit that has been retained by our species, think of the way that hair will stand up on bodies of some animals when those animals are frightened. Long ago when our species was covered with dense body hair, the hair stood up when they became frightened. It still stands up when modern humans are frightened, too, even though we now have so little body hair that it is not easy to notice.

If you want proof, go to *Gray's Anatomy*. However, you may not have that book handy so you may prefer to check the Bible. Here is Job 4:15: "Then a spirit passed before my face; the hair of my flesh stood up."

The various brains we have retained from our ancestors are collectively called the old brain. The remainder is the new brain. Within the old brain are the circuits that contain the reflexes and the instincts. The terminals of all the senses are back there, too.

The new brain contains our consciousness, and its function is to solve problems where the solutions are not encoded in the circuits within the old brain. However, the new brain itself does not have any outlets to the outside world or any connections to the world inside us either. All the data obtained by the new brain are passed over to it by the old brain. Moreover, the old brain has circuits that evolved to solve many problems. So quite often when a message comes into the old brain that requires action, the old brain will direct the necessary action and withhold all knowledge of this from the consciousness. This is a very important point to keep in mind about our brains. Not all the data from our senses get to the consciousness.

Let's pause for an example of this. Our eyes, we know, evolved for use under water. The surface of our eyes must still be kept wet with salt water. We have evolved tear glands to provide this water, and we have evolved eyelids, which spread the water over the eyes whenever we blink. But why do we blink? Well, there are nerve endings on the eyeballs that inform the old brain when the eye surface is getting dry. In response to this message, the old brain sends out a message to the muscles that tells the eyes to blink, and they do. Of course, we can blink our eyes any time we want to, but it would be very distracting if we had to consciously blink them every five seconds. So the old brain takes care of this function for us and does not bother the new brain with the details of what goes on. Normally, we neither feel our eyeballs going dry, nor notice it when we blink.

There you have in a nutshell the reason for our two brains. The old brain takes care of the routine internal maintenance problems associated with keeping our bodies adjusted. There is no need for the conscious mind to know what is going on, and so it doesn't. The old brain has circuits that act as solutions to external problems, too. The old brain may, in these cases, furnish a limited amount of data to the consciousness, or it may not.

If you like, it may help to imagine that the terminal of each of our senses is a switchboard. At each switchboard there is a faithful and dedicated secretary who receives all the messages that come in. Like all secretaries, she is quite capable of providing the necessary responses to many of the incoming messages. She does. But on occasion there are messages that come in, and the secretary does not have instructions on the required action. So the message is referred to higher authority. (We do not really have little secretaries in our heads, but we have circuits of nerve tissue that perform the same function, so let's continue with our analogy.) This is a good system. But it could be a lot better if our internal secretaries were not so old-fashioned—and when I say old, I mean old! They evolved millions of years ago. The solutions they have to our problems are solutions that were optimum millions of years ago, but are often out of date today.

Let's take a look at some of the actions of the lady at the terminal of our sense of touch. She puts in twenty-four-hour days without complaining or taking time off. When we touch something hot by accident, she pushes a button that makes us jerk our hand back and, at the same time, lets the sensation of pain get through to the consciousness.

All this is as it should be. But we have all read of people who were in serious trouble, perhaps in a fight, and who were seriously wounded but never felt a thing until the fight was over. Well, a few million years ago, our ancestors did not have very much in the way of conscious minds. All fights were serious, too, and, if they had felt pain during the fight, it would have been a distraction, possibly a fatal distraction. It would also have been useless to feel pain during the fight because there was nothing that could have been done about the injury at the time. So the sensation of pain was suppressed until there was leisure to lick the wounds or do whatever else our ancestors did for them.

This illustrates how the subconscious censors data that would otherwise go to the conscious mind immediately. The subconscious has rules to determine what data should be censored, and these rules, too, are millions of years old. Not many of us today engage in serious fights where our subconscious cuts off sensations until we have time to do something about our injuries, but all of us have experienced the equivalent.

For example, when a person lies down for a nap, it is not unusual to suddenly feel a number of assorted itches, aches, or tickles. Each of these sensations indicates some place in need of attention, perhaps a rub or a little scratching. However, these places did not just become in need of attention only at the moment that person lay down. The attention may have been needed long before then, but the little secretary at the switchboard did not want to bother the boss with these minor things until the secretary was sure that the boss had time to take care of them. Then and only then did the secretary open a channel for the sensations to get to the conscious mind.

All of our senses get into the act in more or less the same way. Most of us have lain down to sleep and then suddenly become aware of the ticking of a clock or the drip, drip, drip of a faucet. These noises did not just suddenly start; they were censored out by the subconscious for reasons of its own, until the subconscious was sure we had time to do something about the sounds.

However, the senses are necessarily conservative. Any unfamiliar sound is a potential threat to existence. The conscious mind knows that the sounds of the ticks and drips are not threats. But the subconscious worries about these sounds. The subconscious not only lets them get through to the conscious mind, it turns the volume up. Beyond that, the subconscious also sends out messages that cause a drop of adrenaline to be released into the blood to stimulate us just in case the sounds were created by something harmful.

About the only thing one can do in such cases is to wait. The subconscious will finally reclassify the sounds as incidental noises rather than as potential threats. Then the volume will be turned back down. Incidentally, there seem to be sounds that the subconscious is very familiar with. For example, the sounds of rain, surf, and the breeze. These sounds, it can be presumed, were so known to our ancestors that brain circuits that are a sort of ancestral memory evolved to automatically classify these sounds as incidental, nonthreatening noises.

Our sense of smell works in about the same way. This sense evolved primarily to help our ancestors find food and detect enemies. When a food scent was detected, it did not just happen to smell good. Eons of evolution had created circuits that acted as reference libraries. So when a food scent was detected at its terminal in the old brain, these reference libraries passed messages to the consciousness. At the same time, the secretary at the switchboard pushed the buttons to prepare the body for the action it was expected to take. One button produced a pleasurable sensation, another caused the mouth to water, and another started the digestive juices. The conscious mind had only to solve the problem of how to get that food.

The smell of enemies created different responses by the secretary at the olfactory switchboard, of course. We will come back to these reactions later. But as often happened, what if the smell were an unfamiliar one?

You may be sure that all unfamiliar smells were unpleasant smells to our ancestors, because anything unfamiliar had to be considered a potential threat. After a time, however, when no enemy appeared, the continued reception of that smell would not have been beneficial. It would have been a distraction.

So, as with incidental sounds, incidental smells get turned off. Think how the workers in paper mills are able to tolerate the stink. They can do this only because they do not smell the foul odor after some initial exposure. Ordinary people say, "They get used to the smell." Scientists tend to mutter something about the olfactory receptors becoming saturated. Call it what you like, but all senses evolved as aids to survival. Sensory data that is useless in that respect is either turned off or never gets to the conscious mind in the first place.

Now think of our own body smells. These are incidental odors, too, so we cannot smell ourselves unless our odor changes, perhaps from disease, when there would be some point to smelling our own aromas. Many animals generate characteristic odors. These odors did not just happen; they are the product of odor glands in the skin, and these evolved as aids to survival by producing odors that carry information to others of the same species. Female dogs, for example, when ready to be mated, emit an odor that draws male dogs from miles around. This odor does more than just attract the males; it also triggers reflexes that cause the male bodies to prepare for the expected activity.

The emission of odors of this type is not found exclusively in females. In quite a number of animal species the two sexes seldom travel together. So they evolved to have different systems. A male hog, for example, produces an odor that causes any nonpregnant female hog that smells it to go into instant estrus. Odors such as these are called pheromones. They are a big help in the survival of various species since they bring the sexes together and shorten courtship time.

Do humans generate pheromones that carry sexual information or prepare the bodies for sexual activity? You can get up a good argument on this point almost anywhere. Moreover, at least one group of scientists is actively looking for human pheromones with the idea of making them artificially. If they succeed, they will get rich.

It is suspected that if such an aroma can be found and analyzed, it will turn out to be something like musk. Although musk itself does not smell especially good, its presence in perfumes somehow makes the perfumes more attractive, even though the musk scent is completely covered up by the other odors in the perfume.

If humans generate pheromones, it would certainly explain a number of the quirks in human nature—for example, "love at first sight." We have all observed love matches and heard, "I can't understand what he can possibly see in her," or vice versa. It may not be what they see at all. It may be that each is attuned to the pheromones of the other. If humans do have pheromones, they probably come from certain scent glands in the skin. Male humans secrete more of whatever it is that comes out of the scent glands (apocrine glands) than females. (Incidentally, this stuff is odorless; at least, it is odorless to the conscious mind when it is fresh.)

The quantity of secretion from female scent glands varies

with the level of certain hormones in her system. The Pill inhibits the output of these glands, and there is some evidence that wives on the Pill find their husbands less attentive. Then, too, the output of the glands changes with age. This may be why, after a number of years, so many husbands become impotent as far as their wives are concerned, even though the husbands are still able to respond to young girls.

The foregoing paragraph may be taken seriously or not, as you like. Most of it is guesswork. However, experiments with dogs have proven that the body smell of humans is not a simple odor. It is a compound smell with many components, and each of these components conveys information. For one thing, one strand of our compound aromas reveals our ethnic origin. This is not a new discovery by any means. Our pioneering ancestors would hire a "tame" Indian to tease a young watchdog unmercifully. Ever after, that dog would respond with special hostility to the smell of Indians. Dogs can also detect strands in the compound smell of humans that reveal age, or at least maturity, sex, and a few other characteristics. There is also one strand that is apparently unique to each individual and so a perfect identifier—except that identical twins have the same identifier. Identical twins can confuse dogs.

Modern human noses cannot unravel all the strands of our complex aromas. This fact, and others like it, have given rise to the belief that our remote ancestors "must have had" senses that are keener than ours. After all, these compound smells are features that evolved, and they certainly did not evolve for the benefit of some other species.

All this is very true. But humans do not have to consciously receive smells or other sensory data to respond to them. Only data the subconscious thinks is of prime importance for the consciousness to have gets through. Data on the sex of someone near you is something only nice to have, and the subconscious has that data.

However, data that someone near you had a different ethnic origin was vital for the survival of our ancestors, and this data can still be detected consciously. Too well in the opinion of many tourists, who find that the most unpleasant thing about travel is the smell of foreigners.

Human volunteers have been wired up to instrumentation and subjected to various types of stimuli. (Lie detection machines are a form of such instrumentation.) These experiments have proven that our senses are far more acute than we realize. However, faint stimuli do not always get to the consciousness. That these faint signals are received in the old brain is proven by the way the subconsciousness, acting like a little boy scout, prepares the body for expected action by activating various glands, or by adding various substances to the blood.

These sensory inputs that trigger certain involuntary reactions, but that are not consciously noted, are called subliminal signals. The reasons for them, of course, are that the consciousness of our ancestors was very limited and very easily distracted. So the subconscious kept the information to itself until the input reached a certain strength. But, in the meantime, it went right ahead and prepared the body for the prospective action.

Data on threats to existence, though, like the smell of lions, went through to the consciousness quite promptly and emphatically. Data on friends or mates were seldom a life and death matter, however, so the subconscious could hold up on letting the consciousness know about them. Data on food were passed over promptly, or not, depending on how hungry our ancestors were at the time. The subconscious has its own rules about passing data to the consciousness, and these rules are not ours. However, these rules are simple rules and we can learn them if we try.

Let's consider our optical system for some more examples of how our subconscious may seem to be playing tricks on our conscious minds. Our eyes are amazingly good optical instruments, capable of receiving extremely fine detail. But, as with our other senses, the conscious mind is not capable of handling too much detail. When one of our remote ancestors saw a tree, for example, you may be sure he did not consciously notice how every little leaf was dancing in the breeze. Neither do we. It takes a conscious effort to obtain such data, and even then we can concentrate on only a rather limited area.

So our ancestors' consciousness received only enough data to identify a tree as a tree, and this was sufficient for their survival. Except sometimes. That sun-speckled lump on a branch just might be a leopard. It was very important for our ancestors to have conscious awareness of leopards.

However, leopards have evolved to be very hard to see, even with extremely good optical systems. To get around this dilemma, our ancestors evolved to be able to notice not leopards, per se, but places that might conceal leopards. The subconscious receives all of the optical data and scans it for places that look a bit odd or unusual in some way, like a branch, for example, where the sun was not shining through the leaves in quite the same way as it was shining through the leaves on the other branches.

This type of data was called to the attention of the conscious mind, and our ancestors would get a hunch not to pass under the questionable branch. The same system operates today in modern humans. The operation of this system has created a belief in guardian angels.

For a more common illustration, think of the way a woman can spot a crooked necktie or a lipstick smear on her husband at a hundred yards and never notice the rest of his clothing. We have evolved to notice what is wrong, rather than what is right. It is the way we are. This same woman can walk into a newly painted room and never notice what the painter did right. But she will immediately spot every place the painter missed and every speck of paint on the window glass.

We are a species of nit-pickers. Females are better at this than males. The reason is that our male ancestors could afford to take risks that would have been fatal for our female ancestors. Males still act as though they can get away with taking risks more than females. For proof, recall how males and females may have identical eyesight and identical driving skills, but female drivers notice and *heed* potential risks that male drivers notice and ignore. This is why there is so great a difference in the automobile insurance rates for young men and women.

Back in preterrarium days, when one of our ancestors suddenly saw a lion, his or her subconsciousness immediately let the identification through to the consciousness. However, as with the sight of trees, there was no advantage for much detail to get through, and there was potential harm that might result from too much detail.

It did not much matter to our ancestors to know that the lion chasing them had a torn ear or a scar on one leg. A lion was a lion. And a lion was an enemy. There were no exceptions. This is the way things had been for millions of years.

Then about twenty million years ago, our ancestors entered the terrariums, and lions ceased to be much of a threat to our direct line because there were no lions in the terrariums. The lions who had a choice elected to stay on the mainland when a gap formed in the moving belt of trees that carried our ancestors down into the Mediterranean basin. However, down in the terrariums, our ancestors soon found enemies more deadly than lions. The enemies were any and all members of the same species who were not members of the same band. At least, all strange adult males were enemies of all other males, and this situation persisted for about twenty million years. This is more than long enough for instincts to form, and it would be surprising if they did not. But they did.

Today, even though we have learned not to show it on the outside, the sight (sound and smell, too) of every strange male is automatically classified by the male subconscious as a very real threat to personal existence. The more strange, the greater the threat, too. Even when a stranger looks familiar, there is an automatic value assessment of the stranger's fighting ability. We say, "He looks as if he could take care of himself in a pinch . . ." (or) "he looks like a good person to have on your side in a fight . . ." (or) "he's not the type to meet in a dark alley." This reaction is automatic, hence instinctive, hence a clue to the activities of our ancestors. This reaction is irrational in the modern environment, I know. But this reaction was the only rational reaction for millions of years, and once reactions, or any other features, evolve, they will not quickly leave the species.

It is true that modern chimpanzees do not react with much hostility to the sight of a stranger, but humans have evolved away from chimpanzees. It is also true that there are individual humans who seem to have had chance genetic rearrangements so that these persons do not regard strangers as enemies either. But this condition in humans seems to have negative survival value.

However, we are digressing. Many, if not most, modern humans subconsciously classify strangers as enemies. Fine detail regarding the appearance of strangers was withheld from the consciousness of our ancestors as unnecessary and distracting. And fine detail regarding strangers is withheld from our consciousness today.

One modern result is what is called a poor memory for faces.

Another result can be illustrated by a remark I heard a young Mexican make. He said, "All *gringos* look alike." I have no doubt that the boy thought that he was being truthful. His opinion was based on many observations made by his own eyes, and he *knew* that all *gringos* looked alike. For another illustration of the way detailed data is censored out of the consciousness, think how the victims of holdups are so seldom able to give useful descriptions to the police.

Our senses can, and do, pick up much more data than most of us realize. They pick up so much, in fact, that there is no reason to suppose that the senses of modern humans are even a bit less keen than the senses of our prehuman ancestors. We see as well as they did. We smell as well and taste as well also. True, some material is censored before it reaches the consciousness but it has always been censored. The censored material, however, is not thrown away. It is stored somewhere within our brains to be recalled and used according to the rules of the subconscious. Many people who should know are of the opinion that everything ever picked up by any of the senses is stored forever, and, in truth, if the current theories on how memories are stored are even approximately correct, there is ample room to store everything.

Under the right kind of prodding, the memory banks of the subconscious can be persuaded to release data. Hypnotists have been used by some police departments and generally they are able to get very adequate descriptions from the victims of holdups. Problems of almost any kind will cause the release of data. As an extreme example, recall that many people who have almost drowned have reported that, at the time, their "entire lives flashed" before their eyes. We may presume that this revelation resulted from the dumping of the memory banks by the subconscious in the hope that the conscious would note some bit of data that would be of use. Less urgent situations, of course, result in the release of more selective data. Quite often when people have worked on some problem and failed to find a solution, they may think they have put the problem out of their minds, but the subconscious may continue to try to fit the parts of the problem together. If it does, there is "a flash of inspiration."

With training, some humans are acquiring the ability to tap the data stored in the subconscious at will. The most common example of this is called "speed reading." The people with this ability did not "learn" to read fast. Their eyes pick up everything on a printed page, but their eyes had been doing this even before they could speed-read. "Learning" to speed-read is really the establishment of communication channels to the place in the brain where the visual data had been stored all along.

It is the same way with our ears. Some people can listen to an orchestra and consciously hear every note of every instrument. Again the acquisition of this ability is really the establishment of communication channels to where the entire audible data had been received and stored all along. Some people can sniff a sauce and are able to name every spice and ingredient in it. Those people do not really have a keener sense of smell than the average person; rather, they have acquired the ability to know what goes up their noses.

Someday, perhaps, improved methods will be found to help us integrate the parts of our brains. Then educational methods will change drastically. Each of us will acquire a perfect memory, and we will be able to add to those memories as fast as we can turn the pages of a book. We may be able to listen to a dozen lectures at once and hear every word. We may be able to discard all of our desk calculators.

But all of these abilities may have their limitations. Every young kid "knows" how to ride a bicycle before he tries the first time, but the knowledge does not bring the ability. These new abilities may not be of much help in research in brand new areas, either. There is also potential danger to our species. It is as easy to remember false data as it is to remember true data. Our glands release drugs in response to false data, and our emotions are aroused by false data. Nations have been led to war by lies. But, what is truth?

Today people are working on methods to gain conscious control over subconscious functions. Such material has no place in this book, but if you would like to know something about what they are doing, check to see what your local library has on biofeedback instrumentation.

One basic objective of this book is to bring out the effects that the lives of our remote ancestors have had on modern humans. Let's do this for our senses of smell and taste. It is fairly obvious that one of the reasons these senses evolved was to help our ancestors find food and determine if what they found was good to eat. In short, the senses were aids in decision making. The decisions they made affect us today. We can be sure that before our ancestors entered the terrariums, they ate a wide variety of foods. They were apes, or so close to apes, that it makes no practical difference.

Modern apes have not changed much since well before the

terrariums were formed, so it is reasonable to assume that their diet has not changed much either. Observers in the wild have reported that modern apes may eat as many as two hundred different types of food—mostly vegetable—in a single day. Variety is nice because it insures that apes get a somewhat balanced diet. Beyond variety, however, there are some substances necessary to health and life that are fairly rare in nature. Variety alone will not necessarily insure that these rare substances are ingested. To compensate, our ancestors acquired appetites and compulsions to seek out and eat those foods that contained the most of those rare, but essential, substances. The foods that tasted the best to them, and to us, were not the common everyday foods, but the foods that contained scarce, essential elements.

It is very probable that the plants that contained these rarely occurring substances were not always rare. They became rare because they permitted our ancestors to remain in one spot long enough to overpopulate the area with resultant destruction of plant life. For the same reason, plants could not evolve to contain high concentrations of these rare substances. When a plant mutation with a high concentration appeared, it was sought out and destroyed by the animals. Today, as we know, most plants have evolved to contain poisons rather than beneficial substances.

In nature today, as in the past, carbohydrates are rare. Concentrated carbohydrates, such as sugars, are more rare. Our ancestors evolved to have compulsive preferences for carbohydrates—the more concentrated the carbohydrate, the stronger the compulsion. Furthermore, since there was little opportunity to overindulge, there was no need for our ancestors to evolve any restraint in the amounts they ate. As a result, today children who have not been trained to control their compulsions exhibit little restraint in the lengths they will go to obtain the concentrated carbohydrate in candy. Some adults are little better for the same reasons. For an example of adult lack of control over his or her compulsive appetites, recall how books on backward people invariably include a chapter on how the author's loyal gun-bearer/guide/whatever, spotted a bee tree and was compulsively driven to rob it, bare handed, despite the objections of the bees. The authors, eating their toast and jam, washed down with sweet tea, thought that the lengths sugar-starved people will go to were incredible.

If we consider the compulsive way that people untrained in self-control go after candy or honey, we might suspect that there would be even less restraint exhibited with even more highly concentrated carbohydrates. This is true.

An extremely highly concentrated carbohydrate is CH_2CH_3, otherwise known as ethyl alcohol or ethanol. It should not surprise us that our species has a strong compulsion to drink alcoholic beverages, and that we show little restraint. It should also not surprise us that some people become instant addicts after a single drink, and that they will lie, cheat, steal, or kill to get more.

Of course, ethanol does not taste good to the conscious mind. Ethanol is not found in nature, and the automatic reaction of our senses to anything new is to classify it as bad. But it tastes bad only to the conscious mind. The subconscious recognizes ethanol as a highly concentrated food and energy source. And of course it is. In small quantities.

A few years ago it was a mystery how our species could use ethanol as a food since it does not occur in nature and is a deadly poison to many species. Then it was discovered that any animal that eats foods containing carbohydrates will manufacture ethanol within itself, due to the fermentation in the intestines. Elephants, for example, get falling-down drunk after a meal on some foods. Humans, though, produce on the average only an ounce or so per day, but this is quite enough to have caused our livers to evolve the ability to break down ethanol into food substances.

To sum up this chapter, we close with a reminder that all human characteristics, like all animal, reptile, fish, and plant, etc., characteristics, evolved as aids to survival in some long-endured environment. The physical shape of our bodies is the result of long residence of our species in the terrariums.

Two-thirds of our three-pound brains evolved as the result of the social environment our direct line of ancestors encountered in the last five million years. But that isn't all. Everything that any of us knows about the world or ourselves is gained through stimuli applied to our senses. The data furnished by these stimuli pass through the old brain on its way to the consciousness. This data may be censored on the way. Regardless, the data trigger neural reflexes that produce sensations, emotions, "feelings," and a number of other judgment-affecting reactions. Each of these mental reflexes also evolved as an aid to survival in some environment. The environments where our physical and mental characteristics evolved have vanished. Some of our inherited mental and physical reflexes are still of value in the present environment, but not all of them by any means.

Most of us realize that we have some undesirable characteristics. We call them atavistic tendencies or primitive impulses. We should forget these words. All of our natural tendencies are atavistic. All of our natural impulses are primitive. Civilization is possible only because we can retrain our mental (and physical) reflexes just as we can train a horse to remain still when a gun is fired nearby. We can also substitute learned physical and mental responses to our reflexes for our natural ones. But the fact that we can retrain our mental reflexes doesn't mean that all of us do. Many people still trust their "feelings" in every situation, rather than their reasoning. When they do, it is a form of slow suicide. Possible racial suicide.

CHAPTER 13

THE SUBCONSCIOUS
AND STRESS

THE WORLD of our ancestors was a world of extreme violence. From before the time when our ancestors were fish until very recently, it is doubtful if any of our ancestors died a "natural" death. They all died by violence. Those that got sick did not die of the sickness; they became weakened and fell prey to predators instead. Those that had nothing to eat did not die of starvation; they became weakened and fell prey to predators instead. However, our line survived. Our ancestors were able to overcome all threats to existence except the last one. But how? We will take that up now and go on to the effect that their survival method has on us today.

Essentially we are continuing our discussion of the last chapter, which dealt with the evolution of the conscious and subconscious minds. It was not the conscious mind that preserved the lives of our ancestors until they had time to breed and produce another generation. It was the subconscious.

The world of our remote ancestors was a very serious world. It contained many direct threats to existence. In addition, every problem was, in a way, a threat to existence, too. A large ape that took a banana from a small ape was a threat to the existence of the small one, although not as obvious a threat as a leopard. It is not surprising that our ancestors evolved to treat problems as threats to existence. Furthermore, most problems, including threats to existence, had no solutions other than violent solutions.

True, the small ape that had a banana taken away by a big

ape probably did not attack the big one, but you may be sure that he wanted to. Our ancestors did not solve all their problems by violence. But there was almost always a strong possibility of violence.

In the last chapter, we mentioned that human volunteers have been wired up to various types of instrumentation, and it was discovered that humans receive and respond to signals too faint to be noticed by the conscious mind. Many other things were discovered by these same experiments, too, including how a human body reacts when its possessor is threatened.

It does not matter very much, by the way, if the volunteer consciously knows that the threats are simulated instead of being real. The subconscious either does not share this conscious knowledge, or else it disbelieves it. At any rate, the subconscious prepares the body for real physical activity in response to either real or simulated threats.

What goes on inside a human's body when that person is threatened? There is far too much to relate here, but we can touch on some of the more important reactions.

First, adrenaline is released into the blood. Actually, this is not really the first thing that happens. Many things take place all at the same time. Adrenaline is a heart stimulant, so as soon as it gets to the heart, the heart starts beating faster. Fuel for the muscles begins arriving at the muscles at a faster rate. Additional fuel for the muscles is dumped into the blood. The extra heart activity makes the blood pressure go up.

Increased blood pressure would cause faster bleeding if blood vessels were cut so at the same time blood vessels near the skin contract to minimize bleeding from potential wounds. The contraction drives the blood away from the skin, causing a color change. People really do turn red, then white, with fear or anger. All of these reactions, and many others not mentioned here, enhance the body's ability to take immediate violent action, far and above its normal capabilities.

People today turn into fair approximations of supermen if the stimulus is strong. While in this state, humans have performed incredible feats of strength and agility. But all these temporary improvements in strength might come to naught if the conscious mind did not cooperate. To insure this cooperation, drugs that act on the conscious mind to make it want to fight or do whatever else is necessary to provide the greatest probability of survival are released into the blood.

You could say that immediately following a threat, the body becomes, instantly and involuntarily, both physiologically and psychologically conditioned for violent action. But, of course, there was never any need to get as worked up over the problem of a louse as a lion. Then as now, the involuntary responses varied with the stimulus.

Our ancestors survived the problems of their environment because each problem produced reflexes that made our forerunners supercapable of solving their problems as long as the problems had solutions that required violence. We have inherited our ancestors' reflexes. Our modern bodies still respond to problems in the same way. When our bodies are in an artificially high state of readiness for violence, we generally refer to that state as being "all keyed up." Medical men refer to it as a state of stress or tension. Actually it is more like shifting to extra high octane gasoline in an engine. You can get above-design performance out of an engine in this way—but only for a limited time. If you do it too often, or for too long a time, some engine part will burn out or blow up. Something very similar happens in human bodies, too. This something may be ulcers. It may be heart failure. It may be an artery in the brain that blows out. There are many different stress-induced ailments. But all have two things in common: their cause and their unpleasantness.

Young people seldom suffer from stress-induced ailments. Why? Because our ancestors evolved in an environment where stress situations were frequent. Their bodies evolved able to withstand stress long enough to keep the new generations coming. How long was that? We are not sure, but about twenty years seems to be a good guess judging from the bones we have found. You could say that twenty years was just about the guaranteed operating life of the bodies we were provided with.

However, if you are going to construct something and guarantee its operation for some fixed time, you must design it with the worst operating conditions in mind. Then if it is operated under better conditions, it should hold up much longer. It should be obvious that if we treat our bodies as our remote ancestors treated theirs, and fuel our bodies with the same natural foods they ate, these actions will not necessarily produce long life or good health, when compared to modern standards. Animals kept in zoos do not get the exercise or diet of their wild cousins, but the caged animals live several times as long.

Frequent states of stress were normal in the environment of our remote ancestors. But were these beneficial? Did stress have some therapeutic value? Would a complete absence of stress have been harmful to them in some way? The answer to all these questions is a qualified yes.

Each creature has evolved to enjoy the things that were "good" for it to do in the environment where its ancestors lived. The aftereffects of a mild fright "feel good." It would therefore seem that if we flood our systems with stress-inducing drugs, the results would be beneficial. But this situation is just a little more complicated. Our species evolved reflexes that would instantly transform our bodies into the most efficient fighting machine possible for each body.

It is one thing to have inherited capabilities, and something else to be able to use those potential capabilities. Mental reflexes, like muscular reflexes, require repetition to work smoothly and efficiently in times of peril. The exercise of play in young animals is necessary to develop the muscles for future use in times of threats to existence. Mild frights, simulated threats by parents or siblings, etc., provide training for the neural networks, which evolved to insure peak performance of those muscles in times of real threats to existence.

So, since both types of exercise were "good" for the young in the environment where our species evolved, these activities produced pleasurable sensations.

An occasional ride on a roller coaster is probably good for our children. But we must remember that our ancestors of millions of years ago barely lived long enough to mature. They did not get old. The evolution of our species was concerned with producing modifications to young bodies to increase the probability of survival of young bodies. Today, any actions that we take to prolong the lives of middle-aged and elderly bodies should be reasoned. Our natural "feelings" along these lines are not to be trusted.

The drugs that our glands pour into our blood in times of stress are very real drugs. They are not exactly addictive, but they are quite capable of creating a psychological dependence that is almost as bad. Real drug addicts must have ever-increasing doses of their habits. People hooked on their internally produced drugs are in the same fix, because, while the subconscious is rather stupid, it does have some learning ability.

The subconscious can be tricked by simulated threats for just so long, and then comes a day when simulated threats will not unlock the internal drug cabinet. Then those with a psychological dependence on their self-produced drugs may need to shift over to real threats to their own existence. They may take up skydiving. They may drive their cars too fast and get their drugs from their narrow escapes. Others may take up shoplifting, not for material gain, but for the excitement. Others may pick fights in bars. These are not very logical activities for a supposedly rational species, but then no one should expect drug addicts to be rational.

Our preterrarium ancestors were adapted to their environment. We are not. All problems were problems of survival to our ancestors. All of their problems had violent solutions. All of their problems produced within them physical and mental changes to assist in those violent solutions. Today, all problems encountered by modern humans also produce internal

changes to assist them in a violent solution to these problems. As if that were not bad enough, our bodies do not
respond merely to our modern problems, they also respond to
stimuli that would have been threats to our ancestors but are
not threats to us in our environment. These frequent responses, which we might not even notice, put drugs and
muscle fuel into our blood. The violent exercise involved in
solving our ancestors' problems cleared their bloodstreams.
We seldom use violence to solve our problems. As a result,
we are probably in a state of stress for a higher percentage of
our lives than they were.

The sights, sounds, and smells of lions represented a very
real threat to our remote ancestors. Their bodies responded to
these threats. Today the sights, sounds, and smells of lions
will still trigger the internal defense systems of modern humans. The feelings of alertness and excitement that are produced by the erection of the defense systems are pleasurable.
This is the chief reason people like to visit zoos. The sights,
sounds, and smells of all creatures have some effect on humans, and generally the resulting sensations are rather pleasant.

But not always. The sights, sounds, and smells of snakes
and other reptiles can produce sensations too strong for many
people to endure for very long. These sensations are not an
accident. These sensations are proof of a very long and
unpleasant association of our ancestors with reptiles at some
time in the past. When? Probably the time when our ancestors were reptiles themselves. Now we can see why so many
animal species have instinctive fears of snakes and reptiles.
Their ancestors were once reptiles, too, and the reaction their
ancestors had to their cousins never lost its survival value, so
of course it has persisted.

The threat signals that pass between animals apply to
humans also. Predators must necessarily watch their intended
prey closely. Prey animals have responded by evolving to
have an instinctive belief that whenever another animal is
watching them, the watcher is up to no good. Predators are

prey animals at some time in their lives, so predators, too, interpret a direct stare as a threat. Most animals are inhibited from staring at any other animal unless they intend to fight. Not so with humans. Humans have been the lords of creation in their environment for twenty million years and evolved to be ready to fight anything living.

As children, humans are taught that it is rude to stare because of the subconscious reactions their stares might evoke. A rude young man can get a fight up almost anywhere by just staring at some strangers. Now let your imagination drift back a few million years and envision some individual surrounded by a number of others who were all staring at him or her. That individual *knew*, without a doubt, that he or she was in deep trouble. The resulting sensations were powerful. Today those same sensations are present in humans. When they are triggered, it is called "stage fright."

Most predators prefer to attack from the rear. Prey animals have evolved to have a justified reluctance to permit potential predators to come close behind them. These same instincts affect some phases of human behavior today. Few secretaries can concentrate on their typing if someone stands right behind them. In elevators, most people back up against a wall if they can. In restaurants, the dominant male in a group will sit with his back to a wall and where he can see the door if possible. Churches fill up from the rear. This list of examples can be extended at will.

A display of teeth is an unmistakable threat signal. People who have observed baboons in the wild have reported that when a troop has nothing much to do, a dominant male will be apt to walk over and plant himself in front of a subordinate and stare directly at him. Next the superior will yawn directly in the face of the subordinate. This yawn displays the fangs to perfection.

People who have been yawned at by baboons in zoos have no trouble understanding that the yawn is a threat—the subconscious does not know anything about iron bars, and the baboons in the wild know that the yawn is a threat, too.

Usually, in such situations, the threatened one will slowly back away in a manner reminiscent of noblemen leaving the presence of royalty. The resemblance is natural. That is how those manners got their start.

When an animal or human is threatened, its body instantly and involuntarily becomes conditioned to take violent action. But, what about the body of the one who made the threat? Will his body be caught with its defenses down if the threatened one decides to accept the challenge? The answer is no. The act of making the threat triggers almost exactly the same reactions as the receiving of a threat.

Human volunteers have been wired to instrumentation and asked to yawn. It has been found that a yawn does far more than just recharge the lungs with oxygen. Adrenaline is released into the blood, and all of those other good things that happen put the body into optimum condition to fight.

A good yawn is about as stimulating as a sniff of Benzedrine. This is the chief reason people yawn. Not because they are sleepy. It is to make themselves more alert, because the world of our ancestors could quickly bring death to any who were not alert. This reaction is still of value to some people today. The next time you go to a bullfight, notice that many a matador may yawn vigorously just before he goes into the ring. These yawns may be either conscious or involuntary, but in either case, they work.

Let's continue with the discussion of yawns. Whenever someone yawns at parties, we notice that a number of others are motivated to yawn immediately. We laugh and say, "Yawns are contagious." However, whatever the reason for the first yawn, the following yawns were involuntary acceptances of the challenge implied in the first one.

Most of us have seen some instructor become quite upset whenever a student yawns in class. The student's yawn was probably a subconscious attempt to become more alert. Enlightened teachers should encourage yawning in class. However, what usually happens is that the teacher's subconscious reads the student's yawn as a threat and a challenge from an inferior. As would have happened millions of years back, the teacher's body is shocked into a peak condition to punish the upstart, and the drugs that are poured into the blood create a strong desire to fight. Since he cannot walk over and punch the student, the teacher must content himself with verbal abuse and a secret resolve to lower that student's grade.

Up to twenty million years ago, the big cats were a threat to the lives of our ancestors. Their bodies evolved to react to the sights, sounds, and smells of the cats. We have inherited these reactions. But for the past twenty million years, the chief threat to the existence of our ancestors was the presence of others of the same species. These comparatively recent ancestors had plenty of time to evolve to react to strangers as their ancestors had reacted to lions. These reactions were good and proper for those ancestors in their environment. They helped keep the population level down to numbers that their environment could support.

Then, roughly twenty-five thousand years ago, the environment of our ancestors changed again. It became the entire world. Evolution takes place far too slowly for these last twenty-five thousand years to have made much difference in the characteristics of a species. This twenty-five-thousand-year period, though, was far more than enough for our species to have overpopulated the entire earth, many times over, if it were not for the natural reactions toward strangers that all humans have had since the times of the terrariums.

Today the inherited reactions toward strangers affect the lives of many of us. Intellectually we know that the average stranger is not an enemy, but the subconscious does not share this knowledge. The subconscious reacts to the sights, sounds, and smells of a stranger in much the same way that our preterrarium ancestors reacted to the big cats. Our physical systems are shocked into an artificial state of readiness to take violent action. The sensations produced are those of pleasurable alertness.

The first visit to a big city can be as exciting as the first visit to a zoo, and for exactly the same reasons, because in cities we cannot avoid the sights, sounds, and smells of strangers. This is one of the chief reasons that young people flock to the cities regardless of the reasons they may give. It is also one of the reasons why people like to travel.

The constant state of partial stress within the bodies of city people is responsible for the hustle and bustle of city life. It is also the cause of the higher incidence of stress-created ailments in city dwellers. Of course, I know that the noise of cities is given as the reason, but strange noises were only a potential threat to our ancestors. Those ancestors evolved the ability to subconsciously reclassify strange noises as incidental noises and to turn the volume down or off.

Strangers, though, were never just a potential threat. They were very real and positive threats. Any of our ancestors that considered lions, crocodiles, or strangers as incidental would not have lived long enough to become an ancestor. True, some city dwellers today have learned to consider the presence of strangers as just incidental bits of the landscape. Humans have the ability to train themselves to have many reactions other than their normal, innate ones. But it is hard work. Most people do not care to take the trouble. They learn to control their outward show of reactions and think that is enough. Underneath, though, the constant state of stress is cutting years off of their life span.

As a whole, humans seem to go out of their way to keep themselves keyed up. For example, while our ancestors were animals, they were frequently in a state of stress. But nearly every occurrence was promptly followed by physical activity that used up the extra muscle fuel that is dumped into the blood by stress, and the exercise also helped eliminate the drugs from the blood. Then at night our ancestors' bodies had a chance to get back to normal. Partly, anyway.

They might be disturbed in their sleep, and, if they were, whatever it was that woke them had to be considered as a very serious threat. To survive they had to react. Promptly. Violently. Humans are not unique in this. The saying, "Let sleeping dogs lie," is good advice, because if you touch a sleeping dog, it may bite before it wakes up enough to know what it is doing. Touch a sleeping cat and you are apt to get scratched.

The prompt and violent response to being wakened is the reason why most adult animals sleep by themselves. It just isn't safe for them to sleep close enough to one another so that one might accidentally wake the other. However, humans have learned to control their muscular actions. Humans can safely sleep together. They do. However, humans cannot control their involuntary reflexes, and as a result, they cannot help but be in a partial state of tension all night long when they have a bed-fellow. This tension, remember, feels pleasant to the young, but can be fatal to the elderly.

It is easy to see that our remote ancestors would be justifiably upset if something were to wake them while they slept, squatting on a tree limb or in a nest of leaves. But you may ask, what about those times every morning when they woke up normally? The answer is that there could not have been much difference. Our ancestors were not reasoning creatures at that time. They could not just say to themselves, "This is a normal awakening." Even if they could, their subconscious would not have believed them.

No, for millions of years, the moment of waking was much too likely to be the last moment of life—if they were mistaken about what woke them. So they evolved so that the act of waking, by itself, triggered the internal defense systems. After all, what might have wakened one of our ancestors might have been the faint sound of claws in a tree. His tree! So, like many other animal species, our ancestors woke up with their bodies ready for physical combat and with their brains filled with drugs to make them ready to fight.

Ladies, does the foregoing remind you of someone, possibly your husbands? Do they wake up ready to fight and stay that way until they have had their second cup of coffee? Be assured that it is not anything that you may have said or done that makes them that way. It is the nature of the male beast.

For millions of years, all humans had to be ready to fight when they woke up. Many still are. Men, however, like to think they are logical and rational. If they feel like fighting, they think there must be some logical and rational reason for that feeling. There is, too, but it is not the persona of the wife.

It is normal and natural for a person to be ready to fight when he or she wakes up. Yet there are many people who wake up cheerful. There is no contradiction here. It agrees with what we have been saying all along. Each of us is trained to respond and act unnaturally from early infancy on.

Our toilet training is one of the first steps in this process. By the time we are adults, our learned behavior patterns are so firmly impressed that many of us think that these learned responses are natural and instinctive. Our attitudes and reactions to various stimuli are also learned—at least learned responses can be exchanged for the natural responses if we care to take the trouble to make the exchange. People say that they cannot help the way that they "feel" about things, but they can. It is natural to feel irritable on waking, and any other feeling is either consciously or unconsciously learned.

For another example of how people can learn to change their natural reactions, reflect that for millions of years any female would be beaten up, or worse, if she dared cross a male. It is no wonder that the natural attitude of females toward males has been one of subservience. However, as we know, many modern females are training themselves, successfully, to ignore these natural feelings. Too many, and too successfully, in the opinion of modern males who have an instinctive knowledge of how females ought to act around males.

CHAPTER 14

HOW SIMPLE EVOLUTION IS

EVOLUTION is really very simple. Of course, if you read the literature on the subject of human evolution, it may seem complicated. But this is because the specifics of human evolution have eluded human researchers for a very long time, and it is only natural to conclude that anything that takes so long to be discovered must be complicated. But as you have probably noticed, the chief reason for the failure to know a lot more about our evolution is the reluctance of humans to believe that evolution is as simple as it really is.

I have frequently mentioned that survival is the key word in understanding evolution. Why? Because without the ability of a species to survive, all else comes to naught. Also, without much trouble, it can be proven, mathematically, that unless some new feature increases the probability of survival, that new feature cannot spread and become common to a species. Nevertheless, a great many people have come up with other reasons why features evolve, and at the same time, they have mixed up evolution with other natural processes. Therefore, this chapter will attempt to clear up a few more points.

We will start off with some observations on animal evolution and work our way up to humans. It's all the same, anyway. First, let's consider monarch butterflies. They are very pretty. However, their prettiness makes monarchs easy to see. So the prettiness of monarchs may seem a contradiction because birds feed on butterflies, and anything that makes butterflies easier to see might appear to be a feature with negative survival value. All of this discussion is very true; the coloration of the monarchs does make it easy for birds to see them, but at the same time, we are very unlikely to see a monarch get eaten by a bird, no matter how long we watch because the monarchs themselves feed on the sap of milkweeds, and this juice makes monarchs poisonous to birds. Birds do not know this, though, so every young bird that sees a monarch promptly snaps it up. Then just as promptly, that bird gets so sick that its first monarch is also its last one. The distinctive coloration of the monarchs makes it easy for the birds to see and ignore all other monarchs. True, the distinctive coloration of the monarchs is a feature that is rather hard on those butterflies that get eaten, but it is also a feature with very definite survival value to the species as a whole as it keeps most monarchs from being eaten by mistake.

Species survival features are found in a great number of animal species, and they are frequently misunderstood. For another example, think how the males, and only the males, of a good number of species of birds have brightly colored feathers. It is commonly believed that since the bright feathers look pretty to humans, they also look pretty to the female birds, and that the coloration evolved to help the males attract mates. However, if we keep it simple, we can see that the gaudy feathers on male birds are eye-catchers. They evolved to be eye-catchers. When a predator enters the neighborhood, it is the male bird that attracts the attention of the predators. This attention may result in the male being killed and eaten, too, but males can be spared from a population.

While the male bird is giving his all, his drab mate sits unnoticed on her nest hatching out the next generation. Next season she can easily get another male, at least for long enough to start a new batch of eggs. Furthermore, when she picks her new mate, she will not choose him on the basis of how pretty he is, but on how good a target he will make.

That is, she would, if birds had enough brains to think of such things and were honest.

Again, the gaudy feathers on male birds are features with species survival value, as opposed to the more common type of features that have only individual survival value. At this time you may be wondering if humans have any species survival features. The answer is yes. Humans have quite a few. The most common one is an instinct that humans share with many animal species. It is called "mother love."

For another example, let's go to the American Southwest and observe the jackrabbits. Unlike other bunnies, the jackrabbits have rather long tails. The underside of these tails is pure white, and when a jackrabbit runs, it holds its tail straight up. The tail looks like a signal flag as the jackrabbit runs from predators. It is a signal flag; it lets the predator know that it is chasing a jackrabbit. However, jackrabbits are extremely hard to catch, and after the predators learn this, by experience, they seldom bother to chase a jackrabbit very far. This gives the jackrabbits a lot of extra time to spend on jackrabbit activities.

The only hard part about deducing the reason for the various features of animals is to keep our thinking process as simple as the reason really is. Also, of course, we must remember that human values mean nothing to animals. Survival is everything, but the survival of the individual may be subordinated to the survival of the species in some instances.

Next we come to "natural selection" as a process that creates evolution. Actually, natural selection does nothing of the sort. Natural selection is only a screening process that separates creatures with a certain set of characteristics from the population as a whole and allows these, and only these, to survive. But natural selection does not create anything new in a species; it merely insures that if anything beneficial is present in a few creatures, eventually the descendants of these few will compose the entire population of the species.

However, humans have lots of characteristics. Some of these are optimum in certain environments and others may be optimum in other environments. In such cases, segments of the human population may diverge due to natural selection, and this divergence is erroneously called evolution when it is only a sort of stratification.

To illustrate, remember that everything that ever evolved did so because it was an aid to survival in some environment. Subsequent environmental changes may make some features useless, but these features that become useless do not vanish from the species. Our modern human bodies contain many features that became useless in the many environmental changes that our species has experienced. This is not necessarily bad, because still another environmental change might cause some of these useless features to have positive survival value again. And then our species would not have to wait for the million or so years it can take for a beneficial mutation to show up by chance. Some of our seemingly rapid evolution in the past may have been due to this reaction rather than true evolution. No matter.

For an illustration of some feature that became essentially useless, consider that our bodies all contain some cold-resisting mechanisms that create involuntary internal changes within us when we get cold. These mechanisms did not evolve by accident. They evolved because our species spent a long time in some very cold environment at some incredibly distant time in the past. All humans are different, of course, and some humans have cold-resisting mechanisms in better operating condition than others. Some are in extremely good shape. Many people with these inherited abilities have joined together to form polar bear clubs. They chop holes in the ice on lakes so they can go swimming in mid-winter. Now think ahead to when (not if) the next ice age comes along. People with the ability to resist cold will have an edge in surviving. It can be expected that their numbers will rise faster than the population as a whole.

Something like this has already happened. A few thousand years ago, some segments of the human population relocated to places that get rather cold at times. The Eskimos, the

Australian aborigines, and the natives of Patagonia comprise some of these groups. Today the entire population of these groups has cold-resisting mechanisms that are very effective. It did not evolve these mechanisms by natural selection, though, as is often averred. Natural selection was only the screen that separated out and preserved the descendants of the first ones that already had these mechanisms. Still, if you want to call this screening process evolution, it's up to you.

Where was our species residing at the time it acquired these cold-resisting mechanisms for the first time? We do not know, but that does not mean that we know nothing about that time or place. Actually we know a great deal—at least we can deduce a great deal from other features that our ancestors presumably acquired at the same time. Just as our skimpy coating of body hair is a clue pointing to the terrariums, the pattern of our hairs provides clues to the environment encountered before the terrariums formed—not necessarily the immediately preceding environment, of course, but some prior, long endured environment. Let's go on and see what this hair pattern tells us.

The starting point for human hairs is a little bald spot, like a miniature monk's tonsure on top of our heads. The hairs all grow out around this spot, pointing away from it, as the spokes of a wagon wheel point away from the hub. I cannot give you the name of this spot. I do not believe it has one. No matter. This spot is not at the highest point of our heads; it is a little to the rear. Various hair styles may hide the spot, but it is there.

Think how a wet head looks when it pops up through the surface of a swimming pool. True, some people have hair that makes the spot impossible to find if an adult is examined, but the spot is present in infants of those ethnic groups. In short, the spot and the resultant hair pattern are universal in our species. The natural pattern of human head hair is simple. All the hairs point away from one spot, and the hairs nearest the spot overlap those farther away.

Why should this pattern of head hair have evolved and

become common to our species? The general answer to this question, of course, is that the pattern was a feature with positive survival value in some past environment. For a specific answer, we ask what good is the pattern? This last question was answered long before any of us alive today was born. Those old-timers noted that our head hair does exactly for our heads what a thatched roof did for their houses. The straws in a thatched roof are carefully placed so that the upper straws overlap those lower down, and all the straws point toward the highest point. Rain that falls on the thatch does not just soak through, because the water tends to cling to the straws. The moisture on the straws runs down to the lower end, drips off onto a lower straw, and so on, until the drops fall off the edge of the roof.

It is significant that the starting point for our hairs is not at the very top of our heads. However, if we bow our heads, it is. This indicates that our ancestors endured the rain with bowed heads for millions of years. They acquired an instinct to bow their heads when caught in the rain. This instinct is still with the species, as you can easily determine for yourself. The pattern of hairs on our heads makes our hair a fairly good rain cap, but only if the head is bowed. Then the pattern is the best possible pattern that our hair could possible have to keep our scalps as dry as possible.

Speaking of scalps calls to mind the scalp-collecting habits attributed to the American Indians. The preColumbian Indians did not scalp their foes. True, the early Indians might skin an enemy completely and make clothing from the hides, but they did not take scalps. Scalping was taught to the Indians by the whites. The French and English settlers brought their old wars over with them. Each side said the other was the first to hire Indian helpers on a piecework basis and to use scalps to tally up what was owed. Both sides used this method for many years on the frontier. Since scalps could be exchanged for goods at any fort, it was not long before scalps circulated from hand to hand like money. A traveler could stop at an inn and pay for his bed, bottle, and bawd with scalps.

Where there is a currency, there will be counterfeiters. Our frontiersmen profitably whiled away many an hour trimming and pressing scraps of fur to simulate scalps. However, the little rosette of hairs around the place where the hairs start is very hard to counterfeit. Innkeepers and military supply officers soon learned to look for this spot and examine it closely. Except for this, the spot has not had any real practical value since our ancestors entered the terrariums about twenty million years ago. Nevertheless, it is probable that our hair pattern will survive as long as our species does.

Since the pattern of our head hairs was designed to keep our scalps dry in the rain, it seems likely that the pattern of our body hairs would have some similar pattern. It does, but the pattern of our body hairs is a little harder to see. Looking at the front of an adult human, the hairs that you see essentially all point downward, and this is what could be expected of a pattern designed to shed rainwater while the human was standing up. However, the hair patterns on the rear are a little different. Looking down at our forearms, the hairs point toward the fingers. If we put a hand on the back of our neck, though, and look at the hairs on the other side of our forearms, we will see that the hairs back there point toward our elbows. Next, if we squat down, we might be able to determine that the hairs on the sides of our thighs curve around so that they point to the floor only when we squat.

To summarize the hair pattern of humans, all exposed body hairs essentially point downward when a human bows its head, puts its hands on the back of its neck, and squats down. (This same hair pattern can be seen in chimpanzees and gorillas.) This is the position in which the hair of our ancestors made the best raincoat. For this pattern to have evolved and become common to our species, we can be certain that our ancestors spent a lot of time in this position over the course of millions of years. Why this position?

Again, the reason was determined long before anyone alive today was born. This is the position in which Proconsul's ancestors slept.

A preferential sleeping position used by a species is no accident. There are reasons for that position. For example, many species of birds sleep with their heads tucked underneath a wing. It is not to keep their heads warm, either, since this behavior is present in tropical birds. Just to look at this position we might think that the position had negative survival value. The birds would seem to be handicapped in detecting the cats and snakes that prowl at night looking for birds. This reasoning is correct, too, but cats and snakes are not the most deadly of the night creatures that birds have to fear. Mosquitoes are.

These flying pests love bird blood, but it is very hard for the mosquitoes to get past the feathers. There are really only two places on the birds that are not protected. These are the eyelids and the junction of the beak with the head. Mosquitoes would not just make a bird's nights miserable; they would kill the birds if the birds did not tuck these vulnerable places under a protecting wing. Even so, the protection is not complete, as attested to by several varieties of avian malaria.

Getting back to our ancestors, which came first, the sleeping position or the hair pattern? Obviously, the sleeping position. Then why did our ancestors choose to sleep in this position? To answer, refer back to an earlier chapter when it was mentioned that a sphere is the best possible shape to minimize heat loss from a warm body. The sleeping position transformed our ancestors' bodies as much as possible into spheres. Our ancestors assumed that position to try to keep warm as they slept. Over the ages, the hair pattern changed to keep them dry also. (It should not be necessary to point out that it was probably the continual hot temperatures in the terrariums that later changed the sleeping position of our species.)

Mosquitoes and all other predators in an environment are parts of that environment and, as such, play parts in the evolution of any species inhabiting that environment. It is doubt-ful if mosquitoes were any particular problem to our ancestors while they were living in the cold environment that produced the unique pattern of our hairs. But it is certain that there were other night-prowling predators. We can be sure of this because our bodies show more than slight traces of being redesigned, at the expense of engineering efficiency, to make the sleeping position as safe as possible.

Taking another look at this position we see that the hands cover the vulnerable point on the back of the neck. The face is protected by the forearms. The throat is covered by the chin. The thighs protect the belly and sex organs. But that isn't all. The shins are exposed in this position, but the shin bones are barely under the skin. A fang or talon slash across the shins would hurt, but the bones would keep the damage to a minimum.

Our forearms are constructed in the same way. Unarmed combat instructors advise us to use our raised forearms as shields against a knife attack. It is not an accident that the bones in our forearms are located to keep slashes across the forearms from doing serious damage. It is not an accident either that in the sleeping position all of the important arteries, muscles, and tendons are routed through well-protected places. In short, the ancient sleeping position is the optimum position for passive defense.

Just as our bodies have retained instincts to curl up to keep warm, our bodies have retained the knowledge that the ancient sleeping position is the best position for passive defense. If you have ever had the misfortune to see someone beaten beyond all hope of active resistance, you will have noticed that the victim will try to curl up into this sleeping position to try to minimize further damage. Psychologists have also noticed these reactions and with their customary panache have remarked on the resemblance of this position to the foetal position. They then jump to the conclusion that these unfortunate victims of beatings assume the position in "an instinctive attempt to return to the womb."

If there is one thing certain about evolution, it is that all instincts had positive survival value when they evolved. Instincts evolved as built-in inherited solutions to the problems of survival. To spread and become common to a species, the solutions had to work. They had to be reasonably successful solutions. But no one ever has been able to or ever will be able to "return to the womb." Therefore there cannot be an instinct to do so. But there can be an instinct to assume a defensive position and I am afraid that the psychologists will have to be satisfied with this simpler explanation. While we are on this topic, some catatonic schizophrenics also freeze up in the position of optimum passive defense, and this, too, is labeled "an attempt to return to the womb." Possibly better treatment might result if the position were accepted as a defensive position instead of a desire to take an impossible journey.

CHAPTER 15

WHY SO MUCH
LA DIFFÉRENCE TO VIVE

H UMANS ARE a very strange species in many ways when compared to other animal species. Most of the striking differences between us and the other animals are, as we have seen, the natural result of the rather unusual environments that our ancestors inhabited. Each of these differences is also a signpost that points to the differences in environments. For example, humans have less body hair than almost any creature. The simple, obvious (and correct) reason for our relatively hairless bodies is that our ancestors lived for a long time in some very hot place. Any other reason is far more complicated. Incidentally, there is a rule of logic called "Occam's Razor," which states that if you want to cut down to the truth about anything, simplify it as much as possible. Occam's Razor certainly applies to the problems of our prehistory.

One of the most unusual things about our species is the great amount of difference in the appearance of males and females. With most animal species, the males and females travel together, eat the same foods, share the same perils, etc., so they have essentially the same environment. Within these species, males and females look very much alike. It is the environment that shapes a species and it is changes in the environment that cause changes in the shapes of a species. So it is obvious that for a long, long time our two sexes inhabited separate environments. Not separate physical environments, of course, but separate social environments.

Anthropologists would not find fault with this theory. One of the few things that anthropologists agree upon is that at some time in our past, our species began a division of labor. Mama stayed home with the children, and papa went off with the boys to earn a living. The anthropologists are right about this, too. However, when this happened, and how this event reshaped the silhouettes of our females, are topics for bitter dispute. No matter: we will clear these points up in this chapter.

When our males and females started going their separate ways during the day, they needed to rejoin at times, at least now and then. But why did the sexes separate in the first place? The simplest answer is that men went off to work at occupations too dangerous for women and children. Not too difficult or too hard, but too dangerous; otherwise the females and children could have stayed near the males while they worked. So there was an element of danger present, especially in regard to females and children. This being the case, the females and children were certainly exposed to some dangers when the males left them unprotected. When there is danger, animals have very little choice. They can fight, run, or hide. Only this last option was open to the females and children. But a group of girls cannot hide just anywhere, and some hiding places are better than others. We may tentatively presume that our ancestors found and used some good hiding places as permanent or semipermanent camps.

The above is also in agreement with current thinking in anthropology, but you will notice that the thinking is getting a little fuzzy. So let's strike out on our own.

We have an advantage over anthropologists. We know the environments that our ancestors inhabited for twenty million years back. So if we can determine about when our ancestors set up camps for the females, while the males went about their male business, we should be able to clear up most of the details. We can. We will. There are two methods by which we can get an approximate date for the first homes of our species. We will give you both methods; one now, one later.

In Chapter Two, we mentioned that both humans and chimpanzees have lice. This fact is rather immaterial here, but it is important to note that while chimpanzees have lice, they are not bothered much by fleas because of differences in the life cycles of these parasites. Lice glue their eggs to the hairs of their hosts, and the baby lice emerge from the eggs ready to take up their life's work.

Not so with fleas. Fleas do not anchor their eggs, and the eggs drop off onto the ground. What comes out of a flea egg is a larva, and this tiny worm lives on organic material on the ground. Then the larva spins a cocoon and pulpates awhile. When it emerges, it is a flea. At this time, there needs to be some creature fairly close by for the flea to hop aboard. If not, it dies. Chimpanzees in the wild sleep in a different place every night. They travel around a lot, too. So chimpanzees are not troubled much with fleas. The only creatures pestered with fleas are those with dens, nests, or other places, which they visit and revisit.

Fleas are animals, and like all animals, they have evolved to become better adapted for life in the environment of their host's hides. However, fleas have not gone to the extremes in their evolution as lice have. Lice must have a specific type of blood to survive. Sure, if a louse gets misplaced, it will try to subsist on whatever blood it can find, but it cannot survive on strange blood for long enough to breed.

Fleas have only strong preferences for certain types of blood. A dog flea will drink your blood if it gets hungry, but it much prefers dog blood; and if a dog comes around, this flea will smell it and transfer. However, there is a variety of flea, *Pulex irritans,* which has a strong preference for humans, and it is also physically modified for comfortable living on human hides.

The acquisition of a species of fleas denotes a long period of association with those fleas. Furthermore, it denotes an equally long period in which our ancestors had at least semi-permanent camps. How long is this time? According to the experts in animal evolution, it is at least six million years, and probably much longer. So we are safe in assuming that our ancestors found some kind of homes at least six million years ago.

Well, now! So our ancestors set up housekeeping in the terrariums! We had better take another look at those places and see if we can figure out what those homes looked like, and why our ancestors moved in.

The terrariums were in the Mediterranean basin. This was a dried-up seabed. As the sea dried up, the salt fell out, like snow, and covered the bottom. Like a snowfall, this salt tended to smooth out irregularities in the bottom. Then came thousands and thousands of years of dust and sand falls, which further smoothed the bottom. By the time our ancestors arrived, the scenery was remarkably unremarkable. In the terrariums proper, everywhere looked like everywhere else. (Rather like west Texas, if you want a spot for comparison.) Well, this did not bother our ancestors when they first arrived. During the day they prowled around the herds of grass-eaters, looking for whatever they could find to eat. For water, they visited one of the streams that wound down from the basin walls or from the side of a mountain that had once been an island. At night they slept where they were. The males, females, and children traveled together. The males and females looked alike.

Our ancestors were pure scavengers at first, but if you think it is easy to see something like a dead antelope in flat, semidesert country, guess again. It is even hard for people on foot to spot something as big as a wrecked airplane in the desert unless the wreck is sending up smoke. But the west Texas cowboys do not have much trouble finding dead cows or calves. They have help. Their helpers are the buzzards.

The deserts around the terrariums that isolated these places presented no barrier to vultures, so the vultures were undoubtedly visitors down there. In Africa, all scavengers had learned to follow the vultures to a meal, and our ancestors were fairly smart animals even when they were new to the trade of scavenging. It should not have taken them very many thousands of years to learn to head for spots where the vultures were circling. They learned to expect to find something already dead at those places, or at least something in big trouble. We may as well digress briefly here to fill in a little hole in the jigsaw puzzle of our past. Whenever a species must eat something to survive, that species will evolve to where that something tastes good to them. We can be sure that our ancestors ate meat that was not exactly fresh for a long, long time because of human preferences today. A fresh steak, for example, is rather tasteless. However, a well-aged chunk of meat is delicious.

After our ancestors learned to follow the vultures, their food supply increased. So did their population. Furthermore, since vultures can be spotted a long way off, the probability of encounters at a carcass increased. The first band to get to one could expect company. Hostile company. But the first to arrive had an advantage. They could eat until the next group arrived. Eventually they learned to divide the carcass and take it off with them, leaving the vultures behind.

So whenever the vultures started circling low, they triggered foot races to the site. Males could be expected to travel faster than females who were encumbered by babies. The race to the dinner table created the first separation of the sexes. However, when the males ran off and left their females straggling behind, those females and children were vulnerable to attack by males from other groups. Hungry males, too, and meat is meat. Eventually our sexes learned to stay together until the vultures were sighted. Then only the males went over to see what they could find, and the females stayed behind. If another group of males happened to run across these females, well, the females were rested up and ready to run.

In the terrariums proper there just were no good hiding places. However, a group sitting down could not be seen very far. So the system described worked out pretty well for a while. It was still very dangerous to leave the females and children unprotected for very long, however. Especially out near the center of the grasslands or near any of the rivers. Out in the desert that bordered the terrariums there was not much chance of strangers finding you by accident. However, there is remarkably little water in deserts, and water is a necessity, especially in places as hot as the terrariums.

At this time, let's use some facts from geology to help us in our search for our ancestors' original homes. Almost everybody knows that if you dig down far enough, anywhere, you will come to a layer of rock. Under this first rock layer, there is apt to be a second, a third, and so on. Look at the walls of the Grand Canyon for an example.

Whenever it rains, some of the water generally sinks into the ground. This water gets down to a rock layer. There the water forms into lakes and slow-moving underground rivers. There may be a hole in the upper rock layer and the water will leak down to the second or third, etc., layer and form additional underground rivers. This water flows along until it comes to a discontinuity in the rock layer, and then the water emerges from underground, hundreds, possibly thousands, of miles from where it entered the earth. These underground rivers move slowly, of course, but the water has all the time in the world to get where it goes.

Water that falls and sinks on mountain ranges generally finds an escape in springs on a mountainside. There are such springs on most mountains, even those that border the desert. Some of these springs flow on the surface for only a few yards and then sink into the ground again. Some springs create pretty little green valleys very close to deserts, but out of sight from the desert. Thousands of years ago the Indians of the American Southwest found all of the springs in the mountains around their deserts. If you would like to visit one, there is Dog Canyon, not far from El Paso, where the Apache Indians and the U.S. Army had their last battle. But take a guide. It is miles away from anywhere and hard to find even when you know where it is.

The Mediterranean basin is a crack between tectonic plates

of the earth's surface. It is one giant discontinuity that cuts across all rock layers for over two miles down. Today there are many freshwater springs that empty into the Mediterranean Sea, far below its surface. It is certain that there was water trickling out from between some rock layers all of the time the terrariums existed. Some groups of people, crowded out of the terrariums by the population pressures, found these places and moved in. These canyons on the mountainsides and on the walls of the basin were the first homes of our species.

Unfortunately for our ancestors, their new-found homes were already occupied. Small animals such as rodents had been forced down into the terrariums along with the grass-eaters, and rodents generally have nests or dens. So they have fleas. These rodents visited the springs for water and left flea eggs behind. However, the fleas did not resent the intrusion of humans. The fleas have been sharing their residences with us ever since. Incidentally, it was not insecticides that ridded civilized people of fleas, it was the invention of the vacuum cleaner.

We did not really have to go through all of the above to arrive at the first home of our species. Once we determined that our ancestors first established permanent or semipermanent camps during the time of the terrariums, we could have jumped over much of the above. Camps within the terrariums proper would have been too exposed for long residence in those perilous times. The women and children had to be in a place they could defend or in a place where they were hidden. Also, a place with water. This leaves only the walls of the basin and the slopes of the mountains where there were springs that did not flow very far to lead strangers to the camp ground. However, while it is certain that these camp grounds existed and that our ancestors used them, it is also certain that there could not have been nearly enough camp grounds for the entire population of the terrariums. The majority of the people had to go on living as nomads out in the open.

The people with homes had an advantage. They could send out all-male bands who could go about their business, unhampered by women and children. With this advantage, they could wipe out the disadvantaged lowlanders. They did. But then the living was easy for a while for those with homes, and their populations increased. The excess had to move out and resume living as nomads in the terrariums. But when the excess moved out, they moved out unwillingly. After a taste of home life, they wanted more. There was continuous warfare between those with homes and those without. There were frequent population turnovers. This was an ideal environment for producing rapid evolution.

Now, at long last, we can get down to the mystery of how and why our females changed their shapes. It was, of course, the result of a change in the environment of the females. So we do not need to look for anything exotic. All we need to do is look at the environments of the males and females. The differences in the environments will lead to the reasons for the differences in the appearances of the sexes.

Let's start with the male environment. The males went out for food. Why? Because they were hungry, of course. But this means there was little left to eat around the camps when they left. The males eventually returned with something to eat, most probably with meat. But this does not mean that the males had not had a meal since they set out. They nibbled along to keep their strength up until they accumulated enough to make it worthwhile to go home for a while. How long were they gone? Who knows? A day, a week, a month?

Meanwhile, back at the home camp, the females may not have gone entirely without food. The indications are that they did not. They gathered and ate all the leaves, roots, and other things they could find growing around their camp. The females evolved in that direction. Today males generally prefer meat, and females like vegetables and salads more than males.

Because the diet of the females was restricted, evolution favored the survival of those females that could get along with the least food. Today females generally require fewer calories than men.

Because a period of hunger might commence at any time, female bodies had to keep a reservoir of food energy in the form of fat at all times. Today a normal, healthy female body has several percentage points more fat content than a normal, healthy male body.*

Because a female might have to do without eating for a long period, evolution favored those who could add weight quickly when there was food available. Today women say they can add three pounds by just smelling a bakery.

To summarize, the social environment of the terrariums favored the survival of heavier females. But this in turn created another problem. The social environment is one thing, but the physical environment is another, and what is good in one is not necessarily good in the other. If you could visit one of the terrariums and were asked your impression of the place, the first thing you would probably say is, "It was hot!"

The terrariums were hot. Very hot. The heat caused our species to lose its coat of body hair. The heat also caused our species to acquire more sweat glands than any other species I could locate. However, sweat glands have their limitations. These glands put water on the surface of the skin. Evaporation cools the skin. But the skin temperature is not important. What is important is the blood temperature.

Think of whales: Their skins are frequently at freezing temperatures, and yet their blood stays nice and warm. Of course the whales stay warm because there is a thick blanket of blubber between their skins and their insides. This blubber, or fat, is a very good heat insulator, and so their bodies stay warm regardless of how cold the skin is. In the terrariums, a cool skin could lower the temperature of the blood only if the blood were close to the skin. Most animals, however, deposit their fat in a fairly uniform layer all over their bodies just

---

*Roughly twenty-eight percent as against fifteen percent.

under the skin, and a fat layer just under the skin will keep unwanted heat in as well as keep cold out.

You can see the problem that faced the females in the terrariums. If they did not get fat, they probably starved to death between meals. If they did, they courted death from heat prostration. This is a very pretty problem in thermodynamic engineering. Our females found a very pretty solution to the problem, too.

If you have ever slept under a blanket with holes in it, you have undoubtedly noticed that your body heat escapes through the holes. Our females adopted this solution. They eliminated the blanket of blubber over their bodies, making the blanket one big hole, and concentrated the fat in places with as small a surface as possible, so that the rest of their skin area could be used for cooling. Actually, the optimum shape for a container with the least skin area would be a sphere, but there are limitations on what even nature can do. However, hemispheres are almost as good. A lot of fat could be stored in places naturally convex, making them hemispheres, without much reducing the amount of skin area available for cooling. These convex places, of course, are the buttocks and the breasts.

There you have the reasons for the round buttocks and breasts of our females. They are storage places for fat that provide the maximum storage with the minimum insulation. Their presence on our females is conclusive proof of a long residence of our species in some very hot environment. Furthermore, the existence of these things is proof that our ancestors inhabited different social environments in some very hot physical environment. Ergo, our species started having homes, while our ancestors were still in the terrariums. Q.E.D. Do we need to spell it out that the shape of our females is the second time-measuring yardstick for placing our first homes in the terrariums?

Today there are people that have lived for thousands of years in climates that are not very different from the climate of the terrariums. It can be expected that the female shapes found among these people will approximate the female shape that evolved in the terrariums. These people are the Hottentots and the Bushmen of South Africa. The shape of their young nubile females is unmistakable. Their breasts are not especially large, but their buttocks protrude very abruptly to the rear, and for a considerable distance.* Except for the buttocks and breasts, these girls are quite skinny, with almost no fat under their skins. In other parts of the world the shape of female bodies is slowly changing to conform with the changing environments. The subcutaneous fat layer becomes increasingly uniform.

There has been a lot of nonsense written about "male preference" being the reason for female shapes. All features of all species evolved as the result of environmental factors, and female shapes are no exception. This belief in the power of male preference is so strong, though, we will digress to dispose of it.

It has been said that the short, stocky, Middle European female form is the result of many generations of peasants who had plows but didn't have horses. Perhaps this is true, but even if so, the female shape would be the result of the social environment rather than male preference.

It is quite true that men have changed the shapes of domestic animals by selective breeding, but it should be obvious that if the entire population of a species is used for breeding indiscriminately, there cannot be selective breeding for any characteristics. As we will point out later, females were too scarce in the terrariums for any to be ignored, regardless of their shape.

Now, let's go back and question whether males really do have innate preferences for any particular shape of females. Of course males say they do and go on to describe their preferences. You can note, however, that regardless of stated preferences, most males take anything they can get, at any time. Frequently, the object of their affections need not be female.

---

*Steatopygia.

Or human. Or alive. All of this is rather immaterial, though.

Charles Darwin, himself, discovered that male preferences for female shapes is learned. He discovered and recorded that, all over the world, the native men had preferences for the figures and features of their own females. This finding surprised Darwin because, up until then, he did not just "believe," he "knew" that Englishwomen were the acme of perfection, and he had assumed that this "fact" would be self-evident to any rational male anywhere.

How can we be sure that females were relatively scarce in the terrariums? There is an overabundance of evidence, and we will explore all of it, because this female scarcity, then, affects some features of life today.

To begin with, the food supply in the terrariums fluctuated considerably. Each species of grass-eaters has its own preferential grasses and browse, even if there is some overlap. So, although each species overpopulated its environment, each species did not do this at the same time. Undoubtedly our remote ancestors learned the rudiments of animal hunting by disposing of weakened individuals of first one species and then another.

Next, let's look at the behavior of primitives who live by hunting or scavenging. The natives of Patagonia provide an example. Up until a hundred years ago, when food was scarce, they would kill and eat some of their females. Can we expect that the still more primitive creatures in the terrariums would quietly starve if there were any females around?

It is not pleasant to think of, but we can find other examples of males eating females all over the world, whenever food was scarce. This practice seems to come naturally to males. The natural behavior of any animal species, we must remember, is the result of the activities of the ancestors of that species over a long period of time.

We should also keep in mind that the removal of some females from a population is the best way for nature to limit the size of the population. It does little good to remove males, because a single surviving male could hold a population level steady if there were females available. But if only a few females survive some disaster, the population will shrink no matter how many males are present. All evolution is a trial and error process. One way of life after another will be tried by members of a species, and the ones with the most effective way of life will survive best and eventually crowd all others out of existence. The optimum social life for survival within an environment will become the mode.

In the terrariums, as a natural result of that natural, but unusual, environment, the males of every band outnumbered the females. However, it is certain that these males had a strong sex drive. What else kept them returning to the places where the females and children stayed? When there were extra males, can we expect that these extra males gave up their sexual activity? Of course not.

Rape has been too prevalent a pastime throughout all history not to have been a way of life for the males of our species for an extremely long time. For millions of years, all available females were forced to cater to the drives of all adult males, regardless of the wishes of the females.

There is physical proof of the foregoing. This proof can be read from the patch of pubic hair that covers the private parts of all adult females. This patch of hair is unique. Features do not evolve except as aids to survival, and unique features have unique explanations. To determine the reason for female pubic hair, ask first, What good is it? Well, hair is hair, and all hair on all animals provides some function connected with protection. Some hair provides protection against cold and rain. Some hair provides protection against teeth or briars. The long hairs in a horse's tail act as a fly swatter, providing some protection against stinging insects.

Pubic hair does none of these things. But there are more uses for hair than mentioned so far. However, some of these uses may not be immediately understandable except to engineers. What are the little patches of hair in every adult human armpit good for? These patches of hair act as anti-friction pads that help keep the skin from chafing when two skin surfaces rub. This is the same function provided by the patches of pubic hair on adult females.

Every adult female today has pubic hair. Features do not evolve and become common to a species unless they are an aid to survival. Over the eons these patches provided enough protection to make the difference between survival and extinction by reducing the amount of chafing that would result in subsequent pain and chance of infection. But no one male human has ever had enough stamina to prolong intercourse sufficiently to do much, if any, damage. However, a sequence of males can.

Therefore, female pubic hair evolved as a feature with positive personal advantage to females alone. However, pubic hair has no personal survival advantage to the males. They had sex only when they wanted to. It was only the females that had no choice. The male pubic hair evolved, not as a feature with personal advantage, but as a feature with *species survival advantage.* Male pubic hair evolved to become common to our species because it helped the females to survive.

We can find some more corroborative evidence for the reasons for the evolution of pubic hair if we care to look for it. Any sex manual will tell us that on the average it takes a far longer time during intercourse for a female to reach orgasm than for the average male. This is because the social environment in the terrariums favored the survival of females that could service a series of males—and enjoy it. Next, unlike animal females, human females enjoy intercourse during pregnancy. Remember, a species that is forced to do something to survive over a long period of time—millions of years—will evolve to enjoy it. Next consider the relative infertility of human females. Any pregnant animal is somewhat at a disadvantage regarding survival. Personal survival favored females that did not get pregnant easily. But species survival requires that there be a certain probability of pregnancy per opportunity. The relative infertility of modern females is proof that for an extremely long time there were plenty of opportunities. Hence, there were far more males than females.

After the terrariums closed, about five and a half million years ago, our ancestors moved to a place of faster evolution than the terrariums. At that time the large breasts and buttocks of our females lost their survival value. The original drawbacks remained. These features are handicaps, too, regardless of how much ornamental value some people believe they have. The breasts get in the way and are easily injured. The large buttocks affect running ability. So why didn't five million years in a place of rapid evolution remove them? Well, some people might jump to the conclusion that once these things evolved, it might be male preferences that retained them. To clear up this point, let's have a scenario.

One Day in the Life of Elsie Hominid

The time is early morning, a few million years ago. Our heroine, Elsie, is sitting on the ground. She is naked. She is a big-busted, wide-hipped girl. Her eyes are vacant. She is uninjured, but she seems to be in a state of shock. Near Elsie stands a young male. He is also naked. He is watching Elsie. This young man holds a large rock in one hand. There are some other naked men moving around inspecting some dead bodies, which have their heads bashed in. The dead are Elsie's relatives; the living are the ones that committed this massacre. Elsie is not the only survivor. There is a small boy about four years old squatting a few yards away watching the raiders. The raiders ignore the boy.

The leader of the raiders rolls a body over onto its back and then turns angrily to another raider. "This one is a she!" barks the leader. "You should not have killed her!"

The subordinate so addressed shifts the rock that he is carrying into his right hand. Then he growls back. "How could I tell? She didn't say anything, and look! She ain't got no more tits than I got."

The leader of the raiders bristles at this show of defiance. Then he relaxes. The leader is not the leader because of his strength alone; the leader knows that a two-kilo rock can crush the strongest skull. Besides, what is done is done, and there is no use crying over spilt brains. So the leader motions for the others to follow and starts for his own home encampment. Elsie rises and follows without urging. So does her guard. So does the little boy. At first the boy follows about fifty meters back, but gradually, as the raiders continue to ignore him, he closes up, finally taking Elsie by the hand.

What are Elsie's feelings? She had no thought of escape. Where could she go? How could she survive? She knew that the raiders were taking her back to the camp where the rest of the tribe lived and where she would take her place with the rest of the women. Elsie knew that her status in the tribe, indeed her life, would depend on the attitude of the fighting men toward her. Elsie also knew that she would be raped before or as they reached the camp. You might think Elsie was worried at the thought that rape was inevitable, but she was not. Elsie did not intend to be really raped, anyway. She intended to struggle just enough to let these strange males (as if any males could be strange!) know that, if she really wanted to, she could put up a good fight, so that when these males came calling on a later date, they would bring a haunch of goat meat with them.

Now you know the reason our females have retained the feminine features they acquired in the terrariums. These features became species survival features. The shortage of females was one of the chief reasons for one group to raid another. But there was frequently not enough time or light to make a close inspection of what you were hitting before you hit it. It was dangerous to be a male back then; it was doubly dangerous to look like a male if you weren't one. It was not because men were attracted by the female shapes that these features persisted. The features persisted because these shapes acted as signals to make the males hold their hands.

Ever since men stopped raiding for females, the female shape stopped being a species survival feature. It was inevitable that these handicaps would start to vanish from the species, especially in the colder climates. However, evolution is very slow, and the raiding stopped very recently. In fact, some is still going on, but not enough to matter much.

Human males and females today are sharing the same environment, to an ever-increasing extent. Will they, as time goes on, come to look more and more alike? The answer is yes. But there are things that stand in the way, things that evolved in the terrariums, that we have not mentioned yet. In the terrariums, when a thin female got pregnant, she did not often survive. In the course of a long, long time, as a result, relationships evolved between the female biological functions and her percentage of body fat. These exist today, and you may already know about them.

First, malnourished female children do not start menstruation until years after well-fed girls do. Thin women tend to be relatively infertile. Nursing mothers seldom become pregnant, not just because they are nursing, but because the loss of a thousand calories or so per day keeps their fat content down. So the girls of the far future may evolve to look like boys but they will look like soft boys.

The world's population is increasing at a rate that causes it **to double every thirty years.** In the next hundred years, the connection between female fat and fertility may be the salvation of our species because, in times of starvation, there will be few of the well-rounded girls who get pregnant easily and have healthy babies. This is a species survival characteristic that evolved to limit the size of a population to the approximate number an environment can support.

In only a few score thousand years, segments of the human population have diverged to form the races. The two sexes of our species have resided in different social environments for considerably longer. Naturally they diverged, and not just physically, either. Many people deny very emotionally that there are any differences whatsoever in the mentality of the sexes. I agree that they are equally intelligent, but given the same data, they frequently come to different conclusions. I

167

cannot say which conclusion is superior. Either is frequently adequate.

Natural forces, plus a bit of prejudice, which is natural, too, regardless of how undesirable it may be, tend to eliminate minority groups from any population because these minorities are handicapped in competition with the natives. Natural forces of the same type, plus a bit of natural prejudice against the other sex, tend to handicap females in their competition with males, because nearly every job or profession is essentially a man-made ecological niche created for the use and benefit of males. Sure, many females may be able to perform the duties of those positions, but those duties require that they act contrary to their female instincts to some extent. The result is a high probability of some stress-created ailment.

I do not know what can be done to reduce the conflict between the sexes due to their differences. However, no problem has ever been solved by denying that it exists or by falsifying the input data. An objective of this book is to show how many of our modern problems were created by the way our ancestors evolved. The solution to these modern problems depends on some of us and our descendants.

CHAPTER 16

EXTRATERRESTRIAL
EVOLUTION

IS THERE LIFE on other planets in outer space? Intelligent life? Many people think so. Some hope so, and others fear so. Nonetheless, from what we know about life on this world, we can make a good analysis of the possibilities.

To begin with, we can take it for granted that the laws of mathematics apply on every planet, and between them, too. Two plus two equals four here, and on the planets revolving around Denebola and Polaris as well. Natural laws can be reduced to mathematics also; so Newton's laws of motion and all of the other laws of physics apply everywhere in the universe.

The same is true for chemistry. We will not, repeat *not*, find new elements with wonderful new properties on other worlds. Just so many elements are possible, and we already know what they are. Chemical reactions between elements do not happen by accident either. We can determine by mathematics the reasons for each reaction. Although, while we can, we have not yet done it, but scientists are working on the problems and expect no big surprises. For some reactions, we need the mathematics of probability to explain what will take place, and probability is a little harder to understand than simple mathematics. However, it's all mathematics, and the mathematics of probability will apply everywhere.

Now we come to the laws of evolution. These are natural laws that are based on the mathematics of probability also. So, if there is life anywhere on other worlds, that life will evolve, and that evolution will follow the same pattern of this world. This does not mean that out-world creatures will have the same shapes as on this world or progress from an age of fishes to an age of reptiles, etc. It means that the very forces that affect evolution on this world will affect the direction of evolution everywhere.

Next our scientists tell us that the formation of this planet followed natural laws and used only standard materials in approximately the same proportions these materials were distributed everywhere. From this information, they conclude that our planet is nothing special. Without a doubt there are millions and millions, perhaps millions of millions of other planets very much like this one, circling other suns. Our astronomers have never seen a planet of another sun and never expect to see one. But they are scientists, and conclusions such as this one are within their field of specialization, so there is no valid reason to doubt it.

Biologists are also scientists, and they are in fair agreement that the creation of life, at least the creation of carbon-based life, is a natural process requiring only the right combination of standard materials and natural conditions. Of course it is not very likely that all these materials and conditions will come together at the same time. Going back to mathematics, though, there is a law to cover this situation. The Law of Large Numbers. It states that any event with any positive probability, no matter how small, is inevitable if given enough opportunities to occur. (Engineers like to call this Murphy's law and restate it to read: If anything can happen, it will happen.)

This earth was created roughly 4.8 billion years ago. About a billion years later, life showed up. Statisticians may question the validity of results yielded by a sample of one—our planet—but even they agree that it is best to conclude that the numerical value from this single result will be somewhere near the average. So it is assumed that about a billion years after the creation of a world like this one, life appeared.

There are, of course, many planets very different from this

one. Planets where a carbon-based biological life is impossible. A number of scientists have speculated that silicon- or boron-based life might be possible on these worlds. But all life is essentially a series of chemical and electrochemical reactions. The reactions possible with organic carbon compounds are more versatile and efficient. It is very doubtful that natural conditions could create organic life with a silicon or boron base. If they did, evolution would be much more difficult and hence slower. We do not need to concern ourselves much about any type of other-world life except carbon-based life, and that requires a planet somewhat like ours.

The same types of investigations have been made on variations possible with carbon-based biological life. Our blood is red because of the oxygen-carrying iron molecules in our hemoglobin. Copper could be substituted for this iron; it is, in fact, in the blood of lobsters, but iron is more efficient. Small and simple organisms on this world, or any world, can be wildly different, but only at the expense of efficiency. Large, complex, and highly evolved creatures must utilize efficient chemical reactions. They must have mechanically efficient shapes, too. Evolution is a trial-and-error process, and while it may lead some creatures into somewhat inefficient designs, either those creatures re-evolve to become efficient, or they do not evolve further.

So while creatures from other worlds may look strange to us, assuming we ever see any, they will not look as strange as the biologically impossible monsters depicted in some science fiction magazines. When we get one of these out-world creatures on a dissecting table, we will probably be more surprised at the similarities than the differences.

We seem to have gotten ahead of ourselves. No matter, we can back up. There are many millions of worlds in the universe, all rather like this world and all with life. Where there is life, that life will evolve. It will evolve to become more adapted to its environment.

No two living things will ever be identical in all respects, not even identical twins. Those organisms with combinations of characteristics that give the highest probability of survival, in that environment, will multiply the fastest, and eventually the descendants of the lucky first few will crowd all others out of existence. As it is here, so will it be everywhere there is life.

Then with a change in the environment, evolution starts again. Think back to Darwin's finches. When the first few arrived on the Galápagos islands, they had some chance of survival, even if it was a new environment. We do not know the specific probability of survival, but for illustrative purposes, let's say 50 percent. Any chance favorable mutation could increase this low probability of survival in one of the various ecological niches by a good bit. When a mutation increased the probability of survival of some individuals to 75 percent, those with only a 50 percent chance of survival were quickly crowded out of existence. Still other mutations increased the probability of survival of some individuals to 90 percent in that environment. Those with a 75 percent chance to survive promptly vanished. But when additional mutations increased the probability of survival to 99-plus percent, and the entire surviving population reached this level, further mutations could add very little to the probability of survival, because the probability of survival of anything is limited to 100 percent.

Let's go over these last statements again, because they are very important in the understanding of evolution, both here and elsewhere. A species evolves to become better fitted for survival in its environment. Changes in individuals are the results of mutations. The descendants of favorable mutations, by natural selection, eventually become the entire population. But when the probability of survival nears 100 percent, further mutations cannot have much effect. Those individuals with a 99.9999 percent probability of survival have only one chance in a million of surviving more than those with 99.9998 percent. This is why, after a change in the environment, a species begins re-evolving rapidly, and why this rate of evolution slows down after a few million years in the new environment.

As evolution proceeds here, so will it everywhere. In essentially unchanging environments, evolution halts. On this world two hundred million years ago and more, evolution stopped for many of the creatures that lived in the essentially unchanging environment of the oceans. On the land, certain species evolved to where they were immune to environmental changes of the usual sort, so they stopped evolving also. For some examples, look at ants, termites, and cockroaches. It is not time alone that causes a species to evolve. It is time plus some change that threatens the existence of the species.

On this world, movements of the earth's crust generally produce changes in environments. These movements are the results of currents in the liquid core of the planet. This core is kept liquid by the decay of radioactive elements. But, radioactive elements do not stay radioactive forever. They eventually turn into nonradioactive elements. When this happens, they stop giving off heat. The liquid core of the planets will cool and solidify. The crust will stop moving.

When our planet was young, the crust moved about vigorously. There were many environmental changes, some so great they killed off many species. Today, while we still have a few earthquakes and some active volcanos, our world is so old that it will probably never again produce environmental changes that will have much effect on the evolution of the animals. The point being that the amount of time for life to evolve on this or any planet is limited.

If humans were to suddenly vanish from this world, it is irrational to assume that the various animal species would evolve much more. Chimpanzees have not evolved much in the last twenty million years, and in the next twenty million years they will not evolve as much as in the last twenty. Neither will any other species. It does not matter in the least that there are some planets out there that are two or three times as old as our planet is. True, they will have life, and true, that life will have evolved, but except for the very special combinations of accidents that happened on this world, that life will not have evolved to our level of intelligence, no matter how old those planets are.

Intelligence in every animal species evolved as a by-product during the transition time between adaptations to environments. True, chimpanzees are fairly smart, but between their species and ours there is a quantum jump in IQ. Our own intelligence evolved as a result of rather rare geological accidents plus the coincidence of an animal species at the sites both smart enough and dumb enough to profit by those geological accidents. It is not very likely that anything similar occurred anywhere else at just the right time in any other planet's geological age when biological life was evolved to just the right degree. Still, there are many millions of other planets out there with life, and if these accidents can happen here, they can happen elsewhere. However, the best estimate of the number of these planets with intelligent life cannot be more than a few dozen.

Many features have evolved as aids to survival to many species that became handicaps in a subsequent environment. In these cases, per Dollo's law, those features did not just vanish. Instead, subsequent evolutionary steps either removed the features or modified the features to remove the handicap. Otherwise, those species became extinct. We may be sure that intelligence was an aid to the survival of our species in the environment where it appeared. But, is intelligence still an aid to survival in the environment of the entire world? Is intelligence a potentially fatal defect?

Neanderthal could not have invented the atomic bomb, at least not as quickly. Perhaps our species might persist much longer if Neanderthal had been the last evolutionary step. Many people who should know think that our species has no more than a 50 percent chance of surviving the next few hundred years. If these figures are approximately true here, they will be approximately true everywhere. Our best estimate of the number of other worlds with intelligent life now drops to a few half-dozens. This should be good news of a sort. If we escape the doom of the mushroom clouds and ever learn to travel to the other planets, there should be plenty we can colonize where we won't have to fight our way in.

We do not have to consider the A-bomb to see many indications that intelligence and species survival are incompatible. For these, go back to the fundamentals of evolution. It is axiomatic that those individuals best fitted for survival in an environment will survive better and breed faster than the population as a whole. Nature and evolution do not care just what the characteristics are that enable some to survive better. Nature gave each creature only a drive to multiply as much as possible, and those that spread their genes the fastest are the "best fitted." Among humans, ever since recorded history began, what types have spread their genes fastest? The *Guinness Book of World Records* states "The last Sharfian Emperor of Morocco, Moulay Ismail (1672–1727), known as "The Bloodthirsty," was reputed to have fathered a total of 548 sons and 340 daughters." It is this type of person who spreads his genes faster than the average.

With the possible exception of a few like Solomon, the men of ancient and modern times who were noted for their intelligence were not noted for the numbers of their children. Quite the reverse. Today the population of the Caribbean islands is growing faster than anywhere else, if we discount immigration. The population growth of native Frenchmen is a negative figure.

Then, too, in many places at many times it was not smart to seem intelligent. Soon after the Greeks learned how to write, they began burning books. At many places and at many times since, the authors were burned with their books. If you check the news from Cambodia and Africa, you will note that an education may sometimes be considered as justification for a death sentence. The gaps in the world population are filled with the descendants of the modern Moulay Ismails. We should not expect things to be much different on any other world. So regardless of how many planets evolved intelligent life, our best guess as to the number that have it now is one. In another million years or less, even if our species survives that long, the most probable number is none.

Many science fiction stories start with the landing of a flying saucer and the emergence of altruistic superscientists from the stars with solutions for all of our problems. Can we really expect that something like this will happen? We must assume that any creatures smart enough to get here from wherever are at least as smart as we are. They will be intelligent enough to know that intelligence does not appear in a species by combat against the forces of nature or other animals. No, they will know that intelligence evolves by combat against entities with slowly increasing intelligence of their own—in short, by intraspecies combat.

Those supersmart creatures will have become supersmart the same way that we did. Well, perhaps not. There is some very slight possibility that they became supersmart in response to some environmental pressures that we cannot imagine. Nonetheless, it must be expected that before creatures from the stars drop in for a visit, they will have thoroughly investigated us to find out what kind of creatures we are. This investigation will surely have included the details of our evolution. Now put yourself in the shoes of those creatures from outer space. If you were one of them, would you want to help a species with a history like ours get loose among the stars? Since the knowledge that something has been done is proof that it can be duplicated, would you even want to let one of us know, positively, that star trips are possible?

I am very much of the opinion that even if we have neighbors in the universe, those neighbors are more concerned with building fences than in social visits. Whatever our species will ever accomplish, we will do it on our own.

Suddenly, I feel very lonely.

EPILOGUE

OF COURSE, this book does not solve all the problems of prehistory. However, it provides an outline, and new findings can be fitted into this outline as they are discovered or derived.

What remains to be done? Well, to begin with, many people are not going to be happy with Proconsul at the top of our family tree. So, for a start, let's speculate that the very first of our line who was forced into the terrariums was not Proconsul but an earlier apelike creature called *Dryopithecus,* whose remains have been found (significantly?) in the valley of the Rhone River, near the Mediterranean, and in other places as well.

From this start we can speculate that the relics of Proconsul are the relics of early refugees on the African side and go on from there. Better estimates of the dates the terrariums formed may confirm or refute this speculation. More pick and shovel work may identify the specific islands where the races were formed. Further research into geology may tie down the dates these races were released into the world.

In addition to the above, this book is admittedly vague in some places. Additional data from pick and shovel searches is needed to clear up some of these. However, data is already on hand to clear up many of these vague spots. If we had digressed every time to introduce this additional data, though, this report would be several times as long as it is and much harder to follow. So some parts of the account were left a bit vague to keep the narration moving at a reasonable pace.

The most important point this book makes, I hope, is that there are methods to tie seemingly unrelated and seemingly contradictory data together. Anthropology is not the only field that has not used these modern methods. (Yet.) There are many more fields that are still essentially in the data collection stage of their evolution to become sciences. At present, the facts in those fields are tied together with opinions instead of natural laws. The day is coming, though, when some person or group will sit down to do for these fields what I have tried to do for our prehistory.

There is only one uncertainty: Will the work be done by people within those fields, or by outsiders?

INDEX

adrenaline, 130, 136

Africa, 10, 15, 16, 21, 25, 26, 28, 47, 49, 77, 96, 154, 161; Australopithecus in, 54–55

alcoholic beverages, 127

Andaman Islands, 84

animals, 57, 62; defensive features, 96–97; evolution of, 13, 29, 141–3; horned, 96; odors, 117–18. *See also* baboons; birds; chimpanzees; coyotes; dogs; fish; leopards; lions; wolves

antelope, 96

anthropology, 9, 152; methodology, 1–4, 13, 178; mysteries of, 54, 78

Asia, 84, 96

Aswan Dam, 42

Atlantic Ocean, 29–30

Atlantis, 30

Australia, 38, 84; aborigines, 145

Australopithecus, 54–57, 59, 77, 78

baboons, 48–49, 98–99, 135–6

Bible, 73–74, 104, 110, 113

biofeedback, 125

birds, 142–3, 148; Darwin's finches, 23–24, 80, 172; vultures, 154

Blair, Clay, Jr., 46

body hair, 18, 25–26, 50, 97–100, 113, 151; beards, 97–98; cutting, 107–10; as defensive feature,

99–100; female pubic, 163–4; patterns, 145–7

body shape, 56; sex differences, 158–62

body smells, 117

brain, 56, 58, 64, 65, 68; evolution of, 11–15. *See also* instincts; intelligence

Broom, Robert, 54

buffalo, 77–78

Bushmen, 161

cannibalism, 46

Caribbean Islands, 91

chickens, 96

children, 65–66, 88, 135; play, 106–7; as prey, 99–100

chimpanzees, 16, 17, 18, 21, 25–26, 49–50, 57, 66, 92–95, 100–2, 106, 153, 173, 174

China, 47

cold-resisting mechanisms, 144–5

competition, 57, 95

conscience, 67–68

consciousness, 112, 113–16, 129, 130, 131

Continents Adrift and Continents Aground, 28

coyotes, 71; wolves and, 81, 85–86

Crete, 43

Cro–Magnon man, 78–79

Cyprus, 43